CHILDCRAFT
THE HOW AND WHY LIBRARY

THE WORLD OF ANIMALS

World Book, Inc.
a Scott Fetzer company
Chicago

Childcraft—The How and Why Library
(Reg. U.S. Pat. and T.M. Off.—Marca Registrada)
© 2000 World Book, Inc. All rights reserved. This volume may not
be reproduced in whole or in part in any form without prior written
permission from the publisher.

World Book, Inc.
233 N. Michigan Avenue
Chicago, IL 60601

© 1996, 1995, 1994, 1993, 1991, 1990, 1989, 1987, 1986, 1985
World Book, Inc. © 1982, 1981, 1980, 1979, World Book-Childcraft
International, Inc. © 1976, 1974, 1973, 1971, 1970, 1969, 1968, 1965,
1964 Field Enterprises Educational Corporation.

International Copyright © 1996, 1995, 1994, 1993, 1991, 1990, 1989,
1987, 1986, 1985 World Book, Inc. International Copyright © 1982,
1981, 1980, 1979 World Book-Childcraft International, Inc. International
Copyright © 1976, 1974, 1973, 1971, 1970, 1969, 1968, 1965, 1964
Field Enterprises Educational Corporation.

Childcraft—The How and Why Library ISBN 0-7166-0197-4
The World of Animals ISBN 0-7166-0153-2
Library of Congress Catalog Card Number 98-75114
Printed in the United States of America
1 2 3 4 5 6 7 8 9 06 05 04 03 02 01 00

**For information on other World Book products,
visit our Web site at www.worldbook.com
For information on sales to schools and libraries in the
United States, call 1-800-975-3250.
For information on sales to schools and libraries in
Canada, call 1-800-837-5365.**

Contents

Know It All! boxes have fun-filled facts.

Each activity has a number. The higher the number, the more adult help you may need.

An activity that has this colorful border is a little more complex than one without the border.

Introduction

Do you know why bats are our friends? Can you tell the difference between a whale and a fish, a crocodile and an alligator, or a frog and a toad?

In *The World of Animals,* you'll find the answers to these questions and more. You'll learn about the many different kinds of animals, where they live, what they eat, and how they behave. You'll read about animals in danger and discover how you can help save them. You'll also find out about jobs that include working with animals.

There are many features in this book to help you find your way through it. You'll find fun-filled facts in the boxes marked **Know It All!** Look for the words **Try This!** over a colored ball. The activity that follows offers a way to learn more about animals. For example, you can build a bat house or set up your own aquarium.

As you read this book, you will see that some words are printed in bold type, **like this.** These are words that might be new to you. You can find the meanings and pronunciations of these words in the

Glossary at the back of the book. Turn to the **Index** to look up page numbers of subjects that interest you the most.

If you enjoy learning about animals, find out more about them in other resources. Here are just a few. Check them out at a bookstore or at your local or school library.

At the Zoo: 2, Video Goldsholl Learning Videos, 1997 25 minutes. *You will love visiting the homes of exotic animals and singing along in this award-winning video.*

Baby Whale Rescue: The True Story of JJ by Caroline Arnold and Richard Hewett, 1999. *This is the story of a baby gray whale that got separated from its mother and was rescued.*

Changing Shape by Paul Bennett, 1994. *Read about many baby animals that change shape before they became adults.*

Coral Reef by Paul Fleisher, 1998. *Learn about the animals that make up the brightly colored underwater gardens called coral reefs.*

Desert Babies by Kathy Darling, 1997. *Emu and caracal are only two of the many desert babies you will learn about in this book. See also this author's books on rain forest and arctic babies.*

Down a River by Carole Telford and Rod Theodorou, 1998. *As you take a journey down the Missouri and Mississippi rivers, you will meet the animals that make their homes there.*

The Insect Book: A Basic Guide to the Collection and Care of Common Insects for Young Children by Connie Zakowski, 1997.

The Kids' Wildlife Book by Warner Shedd, 1994. *Explore the world of animals as you participate in indoor and outdoor experiences.*

World Book's Animals of the World, by World Book, Inc., 2000. *This multi-volume set examines a different animal family in each volume.*

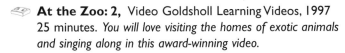

Wonderful animals are found all around the world. Here's just a peek at some of the special animals you'll meet in this book. The map shows you one place in the world where each fantastic animal can be found. Turn to the pages listed to find out more!

ARCTIC OCEAN

PACIFIC OCEAN

ATLANTIC OCEAN

INDIAN
OCEAN

What Is an Animal?

A dahlia is a plant.

Look closely at each pair of creatures. Can you tell which one is an animal and which one is a plant? You can't always tell just by looking. Some plants look like animals, and some animals look like plants.

A sea anemone is an animal.

A sea anemone (uh NEHM uh nee) looks like a flower, but it is not. When a fish swims by and touches the sea anemone's petals, the fish gets caught. A little mouth opens up in the middle of the "flower" and grabs the fish!

Plants don't eat food the same way animals do. Most green plants make their own food with help from sunshine, air, and water. But animals can't make their own food. So they eat plants or other animals.

The sea anemone slides slowly over the sand. Can a plant move around? No, it cannot. Once a plant sprouts up from its seed or roots, it stays in the same place. But most animals can get around by themselves.

If a living thing moves about and eats food, it's an animal.

A sea lily is an animal.

An ostrich plume fern is a plant.

Their names sound somewhat alike, but a pussy cat is an animal and a pussy willow is a plant.

Animals Move

Animals can move in many different ways. They may waddle, swim, swoop, or hop. Some slither, others walk or run.

A clam has only one foot for digging into mud or sand. A penguin walks on two legs. A dog walks or runs on four legs. Ladybugs walk on six legs. Spiders walk on eight legs. Centipedes may have a hundred pairs of legs to walk on, and some millipedes walk on more legs than that! Snakes and worms slither around on no legs at all. Bats and most kinds of birds and insects fly. And fish swim.

Some animals move only when they are very young. Barnacles, sponges, and baby oysters swim through the water until they find a good place to stay. Then they fasten themselves down and never move again.

Animals can move around without help. If a living thing moves by itself, it's an animal.

millipede crawling

kangaroo hopping

snake slithering

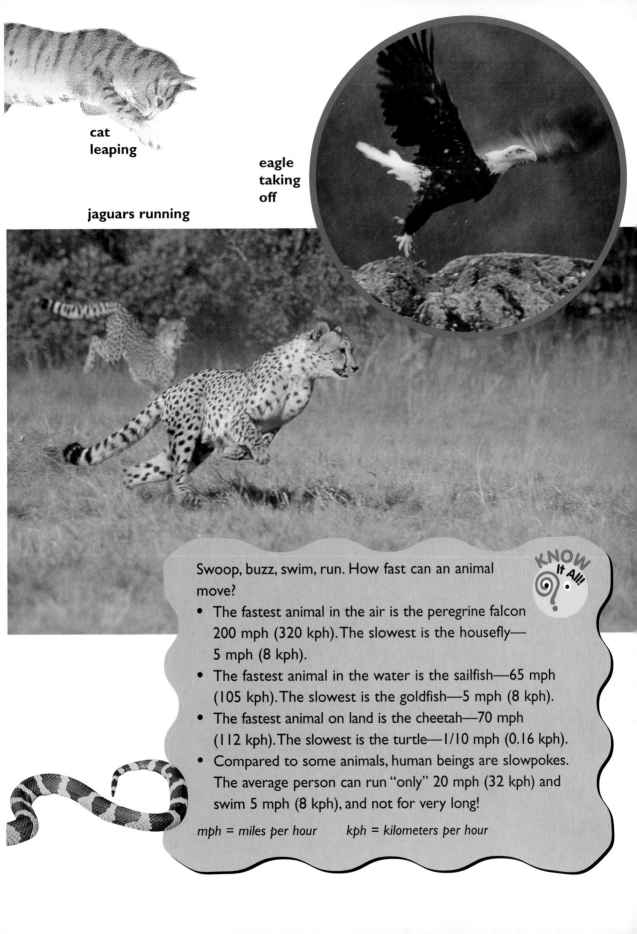

cat
leaping

eagle
taking
off

jaguars running

Swoop, buzz, swim, run. How fast can an animal move?

- The fastest animal in the air is the peregrine falcon 200 mph (320 kph). The slowest is the housefly—5 mph (8 kph).

- The fastest animal in the water is the sailfish—65 mph (105 kph). The slowest is the goldfish—5 mph (8 kph).

- The fastest animal on land is the cheetah—70 mph (112 kph). The slowest is the turtle—1/10 mph (0.16 kph).

- Compared to some animals, human beings are slowpokes. The average person can run "only" 20 mph (32 kph) and swim 5 mph (8 kph), and not for very long!

mph = miles per hour   *kph = kilometers per hour*

KNOW It All!

Animals Eat

All plants and all animals need food. Most plants make their own food from light, water, and **substances** in the ground and air. But animals cannot make their own food. They must eat plants or other animals to live.

Different kinds of animals eat in different kinds of ways. A chameleon (kuh MEE lee uhn) flips out its sticky tongue and catches insects. A lammergeier, a type of vulture, uses its sharp claws and hooked beak to tear its food.

A butterfly has a mouthpart like a built-in straw. It's called a proboscis (proh BAHS ihs). The butterfly keeps its proboscis rolled up until it gets hungry. Then it unrolls its proboscis, puts it into a flower, and sucks up sweet nectar.

butterfly

African lammergeier

South American giant anteater

A ground squirrel has strong teeth for cracking nuts and seeds. It carries food home in its cheeks and "squirrels" it away.

A baleen whale fills its mouth with seawater. The water is full of tiny plants and animals. The whale lets the water run out of its mouth. Then it swallows the plants and animals that remain.

raccoon

KNOW It All!

What's for dinner? Animals can be grouped by what they eat. Some animals eat only plants. They are called herbivores. Herbivores include cattle, sheep, and squirrels. Animals that eat only other animals are called carnivores. Carnivores include lions, foxes, and snakes. Animals that eat both plants and animals are called omnivores. Omnivores include bears, raccoons, hogs, and human beings. What do you think animals that eat only insects are called? Right! Insectivores. Anteaters and hedgehogs are insectivores.

king cobra

golden-mantled ground squirrel

A baby flamingo leaves its nest about five days after it hatches.

Animals Have Babies

All living creatures make new living things like themselves. They reproduce. Every baby animal comes from a grown-up animal like itself. A baby penguin comes from a penguin. A baby horse comes from a horse. A baby beetle comes from a beetle.

Animal babies are born in different ways. Some baby animals come right out of the mother's body. Horses are born this way. So are cats, monkeys, whales, and snakes. And so are people.

Some baby animals hatch out of eggs that come from their mothers' bodies.

Can you match each baby animal with its parent?

1. kid   **a.** human being

2. calf   **b.** beaver or rabbit

3. foal   **c.** kangaroo

4. joey   **d.** duck

5. child   **e.** horse

6. cub   **f.** whale, dolphin, elephant, or cattle

7. kit   **g.** goat or antelope

8. duckling **h.** bear or tiger

9. cygnet   **i.** swan

Answers: 1.g; 2.f; 3.e; 4.c; 5.a; 6.h; 7.b; 8.d; 9.i.

Baby grasshoppers hatch from eggs that the female lays in the ground.

Penguins are born this way. So are beetles, frogs, and most fish.

Many animals do not care for their babies after they are born. For example, some frogs and toads and many kinds of fish lay their eggs and let the babies take care of themselves.

Other animals stay with their babies for a long time. Many birds teach their babies to fly. Many mammals teach their young to hunt for food.

Some baby animals look just like their parents. Some look very different. But every baby animal grows up to be exactly the same kind of animal as its parents.

A baby elephant stays with its mother until it is grown.

Animals Grow Up

The seeds of a tree take root in the ground. The new tree sprouts, grows roots, and produces leaves—all by itself. Plants can take care of themselves. But, unlike plants, many animal parents must teach their young how to survive on their own.

The baby penguin will grow to look just like its parent.

Each baby animal grows up to live the way its parents live. It looks, acts, and sounds like animals of its own kind—and like no others.

A lion cub learns to walk and then run. It learns to eat meat. It growls and it roars. It learns to hunt other animals for food.

A baby spider grows up and does all the things spiders do. It crawls along and spins a sticky web that will catch insects to eat.

Most polar bear cubs live with their mother for their first two years.

A young parrot learns to fly. It knows how to crack nuts and seeds with its bill. It squawks and whistles like other parrots.

Every animal learns to live like the other animals of its kind. Each animal does what it must do to stay alive. That's the way of the animal world.

A mother camel watches over her calf until it is ready to take care of itself.

Plants and Animals

Animals and plants are different. But they couldn't live without each other! Plants capture energy from sunlight and use it to make roots, stems, leaves, flowers, and fruit. Animals eat plants, or they eat other animals that eat plants. When animals die, their bodies break down and put nutrients, or food, back into the soil for plants.

A deer mouse feeds from a night-flowering plant.

Animals breathe in air. When they breathe out, the air is mixed with a gas called carbon dioxide. Plants take carbon dioxide out of the air to make food—and then release fresh air. In this way, the plants get the carbon dioxide they need, and the animals get fresh air.

A moth pollinates a flower.

Insects help plants by spreading **pollen** from one flower to another. The plants need pollen to form seeds and grow fruit. Other animals eat the fruit. They spread the seeds through their droppings. So animals help make new plants grow.

What do you think happens to all the animals in a habitat when a forest is cut down? Many of the animals either move away or die. By planting trees and flowers in your yard or neighborhood, you can give animals food and a great place to live.

19

Animals Live in Different Habitats

The giant panda must eat large amounts of bamboo every day.

A bear likes fish and berries. It lives near a forest stream. A panda eats the leaves of the bamboo tree. It lives in China, where bamboo is plentiful. Each kind of animal must live where it can find the food it needs.

The place where an animal lives is called its habitat (HAB ih tat).

Each type of habitat is special. Habitats in the polar regions are bitterly cold. Desert habitats have very little water. Yet the animals that live in each habitat can find what they need to survive.

The tamandua climbs trees in its habitat.

Animals such as earthworms, snails, frogs, and salamanders need damp, shady places to live.

Where in the World?

Sometimes animals can move from one habitat to another, but they usually like one habitat best. Do you know where each of the following animals likes to live most? Match each animal below with its favorite habitat on the next page. Hint, some of the animals like the same habitat!

1. mountain lion

2. zebra

3. camel

4. grizzly bear

5. tree boa

6. fan worm

7. killer whale

8. penguin

9. scorpion

a. deserts

b. mountains

c. temperate forests

d. oceans

e. polar regions

f. grasslands

g. tropical forests

Animals Are Sorted in Groups

Scientists put animals in groups so they can study them better. The animals in each group are alike in one or more important ways. Here are the main animal groups.

Mammals

bear

Mammals are warm-blooded. This means their bodies stay about the same temperature. These animals drink their mothers' milk when they are young, use lungs to breathe, and have hair on their bodies. This group includes human beings.

monkey

sea lion

Reptiles

frog

Reptiles such as snakes and lizards are cold-blooded. They change temperature along with their surroundings. These animals have scaly skin, breathe with lungs, and are born on land.

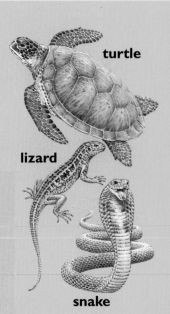

turtle

lizard

salamander

Amphibians

Amphibians each have a skeleton, and breathe with **gills**. Frogs and other amphibians are born in water, but they can live on land as adults.

toad

snake

Birds

Birds come out of hard-shelled eggs. When they are adults, they have feathers on their bodies.

heron

wren

parrot

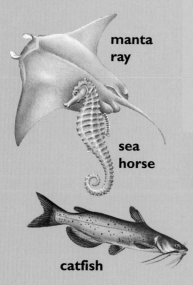

manta ray

sea horse

catfish

Fish

Fish live in water. They each have a backbone, scales, and fins. They breathe with gills.

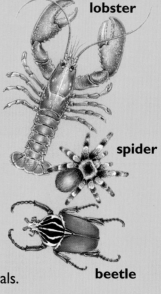

lobster

spider

beetle

Arthropods

Arthropods have three or more pairs of jointed legs and a hard covering over the whole body. Arthropods include lobsters and insects, the largest group of animals.

snail

octopus

scallop

Mollusks

Mollusks such as octopuses have soft bodies with no skeletons. Most are protected by a hard shell, but some mollusks have no shell.

Animals Can Be Your Friends

When you think of pets, what do you think of? Many people think of dogs, cats, birds, hamsters, or fish. Other people think of snakes, insects, monkeys, pigs, or even llamas. Still others think of tarantulas or iguanas.

All around the world, people love animals as pets. In Japan, children train pet mice to dance, and some people keep pet jellyfish. Mongooses are common pets in India. Large sea birds called cormorants are popular pets in China.

What kind of pet is right for you?

Kittens and puppies are fun to play with. Birds and fish are fun to watch. Cats, fish, and snakes are quiet pets.

Owning a pet is great fun, but it is also a big responsibility.

Dogs and birds can be quite noisy, but they can be trained to do tricks. If you want an unusual pet, how about a hedgehog, a tropical fish, or a mouse?

Getting a new pet is fun and exciting. But remember—your pet probably will be with you as long as it lives. So will your responsibility to your pet! Make sure that you and your pet are a perfect match.

Like larger pets, this hamster needs exercise.

Choose the Right Pet

When you choose a pet, pick one whose needs you can meet for the rest of its life. A list like the one below can help you pick the pet that's right for you.

1. What kind of home do I have?

2. Who will be at home to care for my pet?

3. What kind of food will my pet need?

4. How much exercise will my pet need?

5. Does the pet need to be trained? Who will train it?

6. What supplies will I have to buy for my pet?

An apartment is perfect for an aquarium with fish or a bird in a cage. But large dogs and ponies need a lot more space to roam outside.

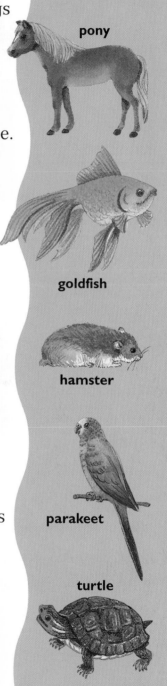

pony

A friendly puppy or kitten would be unhappy in a cage all day if no one is home. But a hamster wouldn't mind!

Pet stores sell specially made food for many animals, such as dogs and fish. Some pets, like snakes, eat live food such as mice.

goldfish

A hamster is happy running on a wheel inside its cage. But some dogs need about an hour of outdoor exercise each day.

hamster

Teaching a pet to do tricks is fun. But training a pet is hard work. Puppies and kittens must be house-trained, and puppies must be taught not to jump or bite.

parakeet

turtle

Your pet might need a cage or a bed, an aquarium, a collar and leash, a scratching post, food dishes, toys, or other supplies. Buy everything your pet needs before you take it home.

I Speak,
I Say, I Talk

by Arnold L. Shapiro

Cats purr.
Lions roar.
Owls hoot.
Bears snore.
Crickets creak.
Mice squeak.
Sheep baa.
But I SPEAK!

Monkeys chatter.
Cows moo.
Ducks quack.
Doves coo.
Pigs squeal.
Horses neigh.
Chickens cluck.
But I SAY!

Flies hum.
Dogs growl.
Bats screech.
Coyotes howl.
Frogs croak.
Parrots squawk.
Bees buzz.
But I TALK!

Meet the Mammals

What do a human being and a whale have in common with a cat? They all have hair or whiskers!

whale

What does a mother cat have in common with a mother bat? They both feed their babies milk from the body.

What does a polar bear have in common with a camel? The body of each animal stays the same temperature no matter how cold or hot it is outside.

armadillo

mountain lion

What do all of these animals have in common with one another? They are all **mammals**! If an animal drinks its mother's milk when it is young, has hair or fur, and is **warm-blooded**, it's a mammal.

monkey

32

seal pup

Newborn meadow mice are not much bigger than a thimble. Their eyes are closed, and they are weak and helpless.

Mammal Babies

Dolphins eat fish. Deer eat leaves. Bats eat moths. Cats eat mice. Mice eat almost anything they can find. But when these animals are babies, they all eat the same thing—milk that comes from their mothers. No baby mammal eats any other kind of food until it begins to grow up.

Most mammal babies live inside the mother's body before they are born. A baby mammal is joined to its mother by a hoselike tube. The baby gets food from the mother's body through the tube. When the baby grows big enough, it comes out of the mother's body.

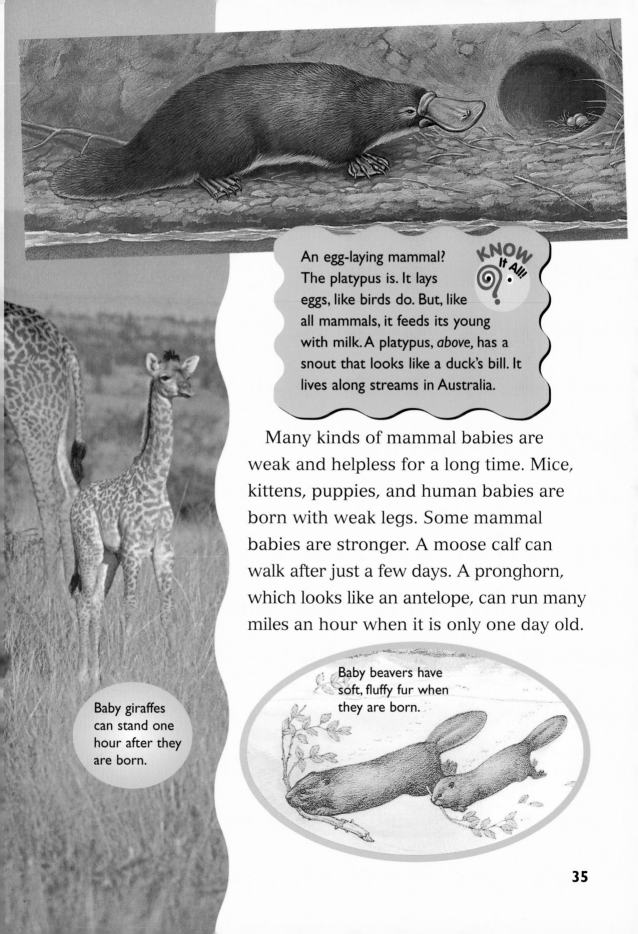

An egg-laying mammal? The platypus is. It lays eggs, like birds do. But, like all mammals, it feeds its young with milk. A platypus, *above*, has a snout that looks like a duck's bill. It lives along streams in Australia.

Many kinds of mammal babies are weak and helpless for a long time. Mice, kittens, puppies, and human babies are born with weak legs. Some mammal babies are stronger. A moose calf can walk after just a few days. A pronghorn, which looks like an antelope, can run many miles an hour when it is only one day old.

Baby giraffes can stand one hour after they are born.

Baby beavers have soft, fluffy fur when they are born.

Babies in Pouches

A mother opossum takes her young for a ride.

A newborn kangaroo is smaller than a grown-up person's thumb. A newborn koala is even smaller. A newborn opossum is smaller yet—no bigger than a bee.

How do such tiny creatures stay safe? After they are born, they spend months in a pouch on the mother's body. They don't even peek out. They just drink milk and grow.

Then, for a while, they spend part of the day outside the pouch. But they jump back in again when something scares them.

Even after they leave the pouch, the babies stay close to the mother. An opossum rides on its mother's back when she looks for food. A koala baby rides piggyback as its mother moves through the treetops eating eucalyptus leaves.

newborn kangaroo

A kangaroo baby is called a joey. It outgrows its pouch at about 8 months old. Then it hops along beside its mother.

All these babies are tiny and weak at first, but they grow into big, strong animals. A full-grown opossum is about as big as a cat. A full-grown koala is a bit larger. An adult kangaroo is nearly as tall as an adult person.

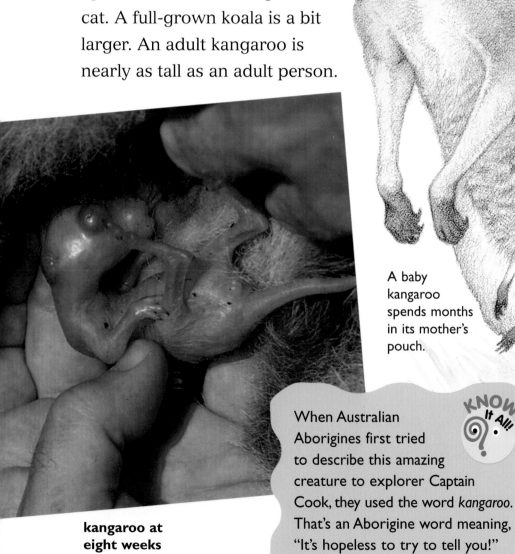

A baby kangaroo spends months in its mother's pouch.

kangaroo at eight weeks

When Australian Aborigines first tried to describe this amazing creature to explorer Captain Cook, they used the word *kangaroo*. That's an Aborigine word meaning, "It's hopeless to try to tell you!"

KNOW It All!

Mammal Food

Lions stalk their **prey**.

The newborn lion cub is hungry. It pushes its way past all its brothers and sisters. Latching onto its mother's nipple, it drinks her warm, sweet milk.

Mother's milk is the perfect food for baby lions. Later on, they will eat meat.

As the lion cub grows, its jaws become strong. Its baby teeth fall out, and stronger, sharper teeth grow in. The lion cub learns to bite and tear and gnaw and chew. Now it needs more than milk when it is hungry. It needs meat.

Some young animals just follow their mother around and eat whatever she eats. But others need to be taught how to eat grown-up food.

The lion cub follows its mother when she hunts. She lets it play with the animal she has killed. The cub tastes the meat. The young lion finds it likes this kind of food.

Every baby mammal drinks milk for awhile after it is born. But mammals learn to eat the kind of food their parents eat.

Baby antelopes, horses, cows, elephants, and giraffes grow up to eat plants. Lion cubs, wolf pups, and baby walruses grow up to eat other animals. Bears grow up to eat both plants and animals. But they all started out drinking mother's milk.

A pet cat feeds her kittens in the same way as a lioness.

When this horse was a baby, it drank its mother's milk. Now that it is full-grown, it eats grass and other plants.

Mammal Homes

The winter wind howls. Snow falls in thick flakes. Rain soaks the earth. Hungry animals prowl. Where do mammals go to stay safe and warm?

Some mammals don't need a house of any kind. Whales don't. Neither do many mammals with hoofs, such as elk and moose.

Beaver dams are often built on ponds, where it is easy to find food.

Some mammals look for shelter only at night or when they are giving birth. Most monkeys, for example, sleep in trees. The elephant looks for a hidden spot in which to have her baby.

But some mammals make houses to keep out the sun, wind, snow—or other animals. A beaver's house of branches and twigs is often built in a pond. The top of the house freezes in winter, keeping out the cold and the other animals. But the bottom of the house doesn't freeze. The beaver can go in and out to get the food it has stored there. Every animal's house is just right for the animal that lives in it.

Chimpanzees sleep in tree nests that they make from branches, leaves, and twigs.

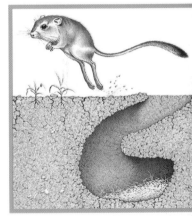

Kangaroo rats live in underground homes that keep them cool during a hot day.

KNOW It All! Many squirrels, such as the gray squirrel, make two homes. A gray squirrel has a year-round den packed with twigs and leaves. The den stays warm in winter. In the United Kingdom, squirrel dens are called drays. A gray squirrel also builds a summer nest of loosely piled twigs and leaves. The nest stays cool on the hottest days.

Flying Mammals

The bat is the only mammal that can fly.

Here they come! And seeing those black shapes flutter against the darkening sky could give you goosebumps.

Bats are the only mammals that can fly. Their two leathery wings are supported by arm bones and spread-out finger bones. When bats are resting, their wings fold up like umbrellas.

Most bats live in caves, usually in large groups called colonies. But sometimes they live in barns, trees, or attics, where they hang upside down by their toes!

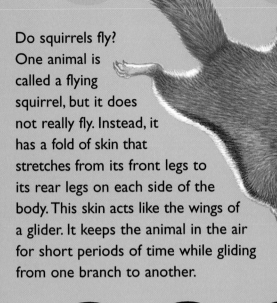

Do squirrels fly? One animal is called a flying squirrel, but it does not really fly. Instead, it has a fold of skin that stretches from its front legs to its rear legs on each side of the body. This skin acts like the wings of a glider. It keeps the animal in the air for short periods of time while gliding from one branch to another.

KNOW It All!

Bats are nocturnal (nahk TUHR nuhl) animals. They sleep during the day and come out to eat at night. Some people think bats are blind, but they really have good eyesight. They have to find their food in the dark. They do this by squeaking as they fly. The squeaks bounce off objects, and the bats hear the echoes.

Most bats eat moths and other insects. Some bats eat only fruit. The famous vampire bat of South America drinks blood. It bites the skin of a sleeping animal with its teeth and then laps up the blood.

Bats fly at night in search of insects.

43

Build a Bat House

Not all bats are the creepy bloodsuckers that some people think they are. In fact, many bats help people by eating millions of truly creepy bloodsuckers—mosquitoes. One brown bat can eat 600 mosquitoes in an hour.

Some people find bats so helpful that they build special houses to attract them. With help from an adult, you can build a simple bat house in one afternoon, but you'll have to wait awhile for the bats. It could take them a year or two to find the house.

You Will Need:

a piece of coarse
  sandpaper
plywood as specified
a hammer
nails
caulk
dark paint
a paintbrush

What To Do:

1. Ask an adult to cut the plywood to the correct sizes or buy it and have it cut at a lumber store. You will need seven pieces of plywood:

One 7 1/2 X 12 inches
  (19 X 30 centimeters) for the front
One 7 1/2 X 14 inches
  (19 X 35.5 centimeters) for the back
Two 5 3/4 X 12 inches
  (14.5 X 30 centimeters) for the sides
One 7 1/2 X 10 1/2 inches
  (19 X 26.5 centimeters) for the top
One 3 1/2 X 7 1/2 inches
  (9 X 19 centimeters) for the bottom
One 7 1/2 X 9 inches
  (19 X 23 centimeters) for the divider

2. Roughen all inner surfaces with the sandpaper. This gives bats a good grip.

3. Ask an adult to help you nail the pieces of wood together, using the diagram shown here.

4. Ask an adult to help you fill the cracks with caulk. Paint all outside surfaces with two or three coats of dark paint.

5. Find a good spot for your bat house, near a source of water. The bat house should be hung 12 to 15 feet (3.6 to 4.5 meters) above the ground. Place it in a spot that is sheltered from the wind.

Bats can move their flexible wings to do acrobatic stunts in the air. But on land, they are flops! Bats' legs are so small and weak that they can only crawl.

Mammals in the Sea

Most kinds of mammals live on land. But seals, whales, and a few other mammals live in the sea. They can stay underwater for a long time, but these mammals breathe air through their lungs. They rise above the water to breathe.

Whales look so much like **fish** that many people think they are fish. But they are mammals. They have hair, they are warm-blooded, and their babies drink mother's milk. Dolphins and porpoises are small whales.

Seals, sea lions, and walruses are mammals that spend much of

Killer whales are mammals that live in the ocean. This 3-day-old killer whale is drinking milk from its mother.

Elephant seals spend much of their time in the water, but they breathe with lungs like other mammals.

46

Dolphins and porpoises belong to the same family, but they are not the same animal. How can you tell the difference between a dolphin and a porpoise? A dolphin has a pointy snout, cone-shaped teeth, and a sharply sloping forehead. A porpoise has a rounded snout, flat teeth, and a gently sloping forehead. Also, porpoises are smaller than dolphins.

dolphin

porpoise

their time in the water and some time on land. When they come onto land, they waddle about on their fins.

Another group of sea mammals includes dugongs and manatees, which are sometimes called sea cows. These animals look a bit like walruses without tusks. Instead of hind flippers, each of these animals has a wide, flattened tail.

dugong

manatee

A right whale swims with its calf.

The Largest Mammal

A humpback whale swims near the top of the water. From time to time, it comes up for fresh air, filling its lungs. Then the whale dives down again. A few minutes later, it surfaces once more, and *whoosh!* the whale blows used air through the blowhole on top of its head. It breathes in again and dives.

Whales live in the water and look like fish, but they are really mammals. They are warm-blooded and feed their babies with mother's milk. They don't have **gills** like fish—they have lungs. That's why they must come to the surface for air.

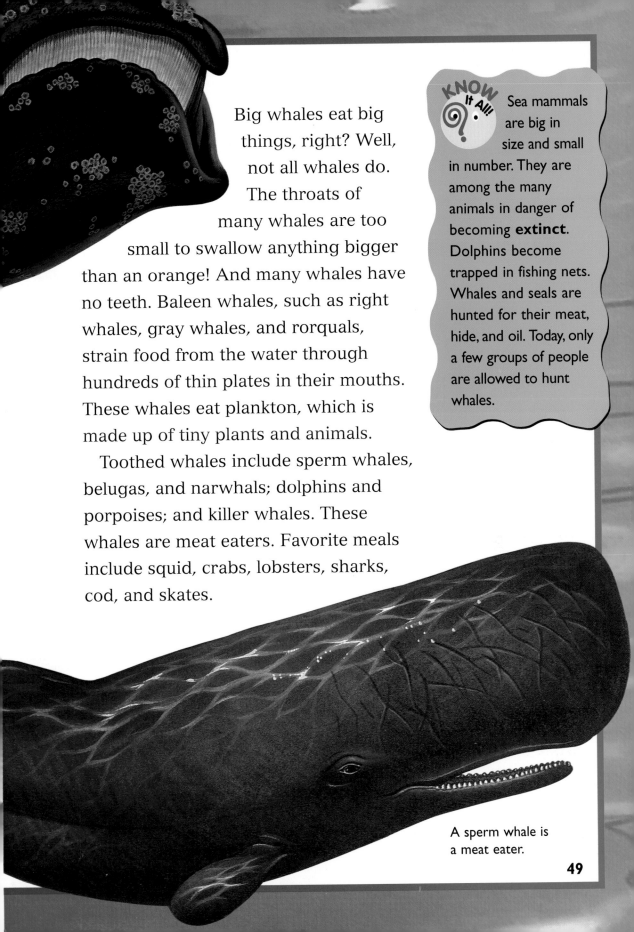

Big whales eat big things, right? Well, not all whales do. The throats of many whales are too small to swallow anything bigger than an orange! And many whales have no teeth. Baleen whales, such as right whales, gray whales, and rorquals, strain food from the water through hundreds of thin plates in their mouths. These whales eat plankton, which is made up of tiny plants and animals.

Toothed whales include sperm whales, belugas, and narwhals; dolphins and porpoises; and killer whales. These whales are meat eaters. Favorite meals include squid, crabs, lobsters, sharks, cod, and skates.

KNOW It All!

Sea mammals are big in size and small in number. They are among the many animals in danger of becoming **extinct**. Dolphins become trapped in fishing nets. Whales and seals are hunted for their meat, hide, and oil. Today, only a few groups of people are allowed to hunt whales.

A sperm whale is a meat eater.

49

Meet the Birds

peacock

Do you know what makes a **bird** different from any other animal?

Not its wings. Some other animals have wings, too.

Not its bill. Some other animals have bills, too.

hummingbird

Not its eggs. Many other animals lay eggs. Not the fact that it can fly. Some birds can't fly. Give up?

bald eagle

Feathers! All birds have feathers. In fact, birds are the only animals that have feathers.

So if it has feathers, it's a bird!

masked lovebirds

great horned owl

Bird Nests

It's springtime. A bird flies by with a piece of red string in its mouth. Soon it flies by again with a twig. What is it doing? The bird is getting ready to build its nest. The nest is where the mother bird will lay her eggs. After the chicks hatch, they will stay in the nest until they grow up.

Different kinds of birds build different kinds of nests. Many birds make nests in trees. Some of these are layers of twigs piled together. Others are like bowls made of mud and grass. Nests can also be holes in tree trunks, or hanging pouches or sacs made of woven twigs and grass.

A blackbird builds a bowl-shaped nest in a tree.

European kingfishers nest in river banks.

The nest of the rufous ovenbird is made of mud and grass and looks like a clay oven.

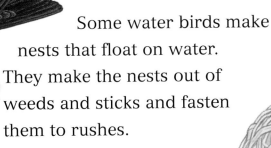

Some water birds make nests that float on water. They make the nests out of weeds and sticks and fasten them to rushes.

Some birds don't make nests at all. Some sea birds lay their eggs on a ledge on the side of a cliff. Other birds lay their eggs in holes in the ground. And some birds lay their eggs in the nests of other birds.

A weaverbird uses its bill to weave a hanging nest of grass and sticks.

An oriole builds a nest that looks like a pouch hanging from a tree limb.

From Egg to Baby Bird

The baby ostrich on the right has been out of its egg for several minutes. In a moment, the other baby ostrich will push itself all the way out.

This baby bird is using its egg tooth to break out of its shell.

Inside an egg, a tiny baby bird is curled up in a ball. Its head is bigger than its body. Its eyes are closed. All the food it needs is inside the egg. The baby bird has grown so much that it fills up the egg. It is ready to hatch.

The baby bird begins to move inside the egg. The eggshell cracks, the crack grows bigger, and bits of the shell fall off. Soon there is a big hole. The baby bird wiggles through the hole. A new life has begun.

Match each egg with its owner.

TRY THIS!
1

1. chicken
2. hummingbird
3. ostrich

Answers: 1.b; 2.c; 3.a.

a.

b.

c.

When some kinds of birds hatch, they are helpless. Their eyes are still closed and they have no feathers. They can't stand on their tiny, weak legs. Birds such as robins and nuthatches are helpless for weeks after they hatch. They need their mothers to feed them and keep them warm. But other kinds of birds can see, walk, and hunt for food soon after they hatch, even though they cannot fly yet. Two days after hatching, a duckling can run, swim, and find food.

Young robins leave the nest about 15 days after they hatch.

Feathers and Wings

You know that all birds have feathers. Some feathers are quite beautiful. But what are feathers for? Feathers help most birds fly, but they are important for other reasons, too.

In cold weather, a bird's feathers make a warm winter coat. The bird fluffs up its feathers to keep its body warm. For some birds, waterproof feathers act like a raincoat. These birds can swim and dive without getting too wet and sinking.

The colors of feathers can be important, too. Bright colors help some birds attract mates. Other colors make birds blend in with their **habitat** so they are hard to see. Then hungry enemies won't notice them.

All birds have wings. Wings are for flying, of course, and most birds can fly.

The albatross has long, pointed wings. It can glide for hours without having to flap its wings.

The swift has narrow, pointed wings, just right for fast flying and quick turns.

The pheasant has broad, rounded wings. It can take off quickly if it sees danger.

A bird's wings are thin and very light. They are nothing but a few little bones and small muscles covered with thin skin and feathers.

Birds' wings aren't all the same, however. The kind of wings a bird has depends mainly on the bird's way of life.

The male quetzal has a big, beautiful tail for attracting a mate.

These crowned cranes have bright feathers and pretty tufts on the tops of their heads.

KNOW It All!

Most birds fly, but some birds move in different ways.

A penguin's wings are like a seal's flippers. Penguins use their wings to swim. These birds can swim as well as fish can, but penguins do not fly.

The wings of ostriches and kiwis are too small to lift their big bodies into the air. These birds can't fly, but they are excellent runners. An ostrich can run up to 40 miles (64 kilometers) an hour!

Baby Bird's First Flight

A baby swift is getting ready to fly. Ever since it hatched, its feathers have been getting longer. Its wings have been growing stronger. Now, the little bird is ready.

It hops to the edge of the nest. Even though it has never flown, the swift knows just what to do. It spreads its wings and pushes itself off the nest with its legs. Air pushes up on the swift's wings and holds the little bird up. The swift begins to flap its wings. Feathers on the ends of the wings spread out and twist. This pulls air under each wing and pulls the swift forward.

take-off

upstroke

downstroke

landing

This sparrow is now an expert flier. As it flaps its wings during flight, some of the wing feathers twist back and forth. This pushes the bird through the air.

Now the little swift is tired. It lands by spreading out its wings and tail as a brake.

Many birds can fly the very first time they try. Some birds, such as sparrows, need a little practice. They flutter weakly out of the nest. Before they can really fly, they hop about on the ground, flapping their wings for a few days.

Shovels, Nutcrackers, and Spears

Whether a bird eats insects, worms, or berries, its bill or beak helps it get the food it wants. For most birds, its bill is a special tool that is the right shape. In fact, the bills of many birds work just like tools you may have at home. See if you can match the tools in the box to the birds whose beaks resemble them.

1. A spoonbill wades by the seashore with its head underwater. It swings its head from side to side and shovels tiny fish and other food from the mud and water into its mouth.

2. A heron also gets its food in the water. It spears fish, lifts them out of the water, and swallows them.

3. A parrot can crack open nuts and seeds easily with its big, strong bill.

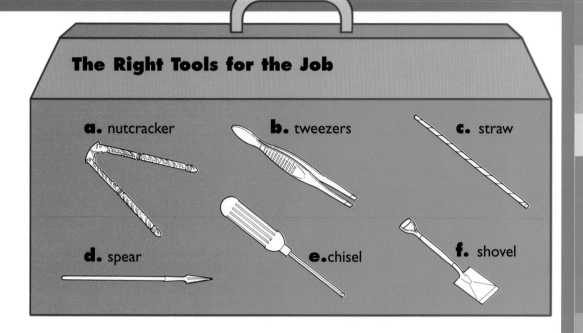

The Right Tools for the Job

a. nutcracker

b. tweezers

c. straw

d. spear

e. chisel

f. shovel

4. A sparrow eats seeds it finds on the ground. Its bill makes them easy to pick up.

5. A woodpecker hammers its bill against a tree to make a hole in the bark. Then the woodpecker can eat the insects underneath.

6. A hummingbird sticks its bill deep into a flower. Its long tongue sips up nectar.

Answers:
1.f; 2.d; 3.a; 4.b;
5.e; 6.c.

Feet Fit for the Job

Would you be able to grasp a tree branch with your toes and then fall asleep, without falling? No, because your feet are not made for living in trees.

Birds have feet that suit their way of life. Birds that perch on branches have toes that curl around the branch to give a tight grip. The grip is so tight that the bird doesn't fall off even when it sleeps.

Birds that find their food in the ground have short, blunt toes like tiny rakes. They scratch the ground to turn up insects and seeds. Ducks, geese, and swans have feet like paddles to help them swim in water. Birds of **prey**, which eat small animals, have sharp, curved claws—just right for grabbing the creatures they hunt.

When the blue jay perches on a twig, it uses its front toes like fingers and each of its back toes like a thumb.

The blue-footed booby has webbed feet that work like paddles in the water.

The golden eagle uses its long, sharp claws to grab small animals and carry the food to its nest.

Each bird's feet are specially suited to its way of life.

KNOW It All!

woodpecker

blue jay

cassowary

eagle

blue-footed booby

The woodpecker's back toes help the bird grip surfaces.

Climbing birds, like parrots and woodpeckers, have two toes pointing forward and two toes pointing backward. Cassowaries and most other fast-running birds have three toes on each foot.

An eared grebe dives for its food.

Birds that Dive, Dabble, and Clip

Did you ever swim wearing flippers? If so, you know that they help you swim faster. Flippers are like the webbed feet of ducks, geese, and swans. Webbed feet are like paddles. They push lots of water, so the bird can move faster.

Ducks, geese, and swans are all waterfowl. They spend most of their time in lakes, ponds, rivers, or the sea.

The black swan and the burdekin shelduck, *below*, live in Australia and New Zealand.

Different kinds of waterfowl have different ways of getting their food. Some kinds of ducks, such as mallards, wigeons, and teals, are known as dabbling ducks. To get food—water insects, snails, and water plants—a dabbling duck puts its head underwater. Its feet and tail stick straight up in the air. Swans feed this way too, but they eat mostly plants.

mallards dabbling

Ducks such as pochards, canvasbacks, and grebes are known as diving ducks. They dive underwater and eat mostly water plants.

Geese usually feed on land. They like grass, seeds, and plants. Their bills can clip off the tops of plants as neatly as a pair of scissors.

Colorful mandarin ducks often perch in trees when they aren't swimming.

TRY THIS!

1

Can you guess what each kind of waterfowl is called?

1. male duck
2. female duck
3. baby duck
4. group of ducks
5. male goose
6. female goose
7. baby goose
8. group of flying geese
9. male swan
10. female swan
11. baby swan

a. duckling
b. gaggle
c. gander
d. goose
e. cob
f. pen
g. drake
h. flock
i. duck
j. cygnet
k. gosling

Answers: 1.g; 2.i; 3.a; 4.h; 5.c; 6.d; 7.k; 8.b; 9.e; 10.f; 11.j.

Meet the Reptiles and the Amphibians

The European green toad is an amphibian.

Have you ever seen a big, fat frog? Did its bulging eyes and raspy croak make you laugh? Have you ever seen a tiny garden snake zipping through the grass? Were you amazed at how fast it could travel with no feet?

Snakes and frogs belong to two groups of animals called **reptiles** and **amphibians** (am FIHB ee uhnz).

Amphibians and reptiles slither, scamper, hop, or swim. Some hiss, some croak, and some make no sound at all. Some amphibians have scaly skin that feels like tree bark. Some snakes have skin that feels like warm glass. Some frogs are slimy, but most snakes are not.

The spotted salamander is an amphibian.

The green sea turtle is a reptile.

Amphibians and reptiles live all over the world—in woodland forests and rain forests, the Australian outback and the African plains, and maybe in your own backyard.

The python
is a reptile.

What Is a Reptile?

Suppose you found some eggs lying on the ground. Now suppose that some little creatures with scales hatched out of them. What kind of animal would they be?

Could they be **fish**? Fish have scaly skin, but fish eggs do not have hard shells. Besides, most fish lay their eggs in water. So they could not be fish.

python

tuatara

Could they be **birds**? Birds lay eggs, too. But birds don't have such scaly skin. So they could not be birds.

They must be **reptiles**. Only reptiles have scaly skin and lay their eggs on land. Alligators, crocodiles, lizards, snakes, turtles, and tuataras (too uh TAH ruhs) are reptiles.

All reptiles have scales. They lay their eggs on land.

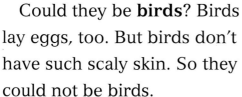

iguana

Hide-and-Seek with the Sun

It's the middle of the night in the desert. A small lizard lies almost covered with sand. Only its head sticks out. It is using the sand like a blanket to keep its body warm during the cool night.

When the sun comes up, the lizard crawls out of the sand. It moves very slowly because it is still cold. It lies on a rock for a long time, letting the sun warm it. When its body is warm enough, the lizard dashes off to look for food.

At night, a lizard uses the sand like a blanket to keep warm.

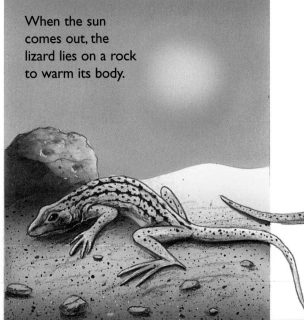

When the sun comes out, the lizard lies on a rock to warm its body.

Lizards and all other reptiles are **cold-blooded**. Their bodies get just as hot or cold as the air or water around them. If their bodies get cold, reptiles can't move well. If they get too hot, reptiles die. So reptiles must spend their time playing hide-and-seek with the sun. If they are cold, they lie in warm sunshine. If they are hot, they hurry into the shade.

A reptile that lives where winters are cold moves more and more slowly as cold weather comes. The reptile curls up in the warmest hole it can find. Soon its body grows cold and stiff. It cannot move at all. Only when warm weather returns can the reptile move again.

When the lizard feels warm enough, it hunts for a meal.

During the hottest part of the day, the lizard shades itself under a rock to stay cool.

Turtles and Tortoises

Turtles and tortoises are reptiles with shells on their backs. Most can pull their heads, legs, and tails inside the shell for protection.

Many turtles spend a lot of time in the water. They can swim much better than they can walk. The sea turtle spends almost all its time in the water and has strong flippers for swimming. These turtles eat animals and plants.

Tortoises are turtles that live only on land. They have clublike legs for walking

The turtle is the only reptile with a shell.

This star tortoise from Sri Lanka has thick, stumpy legs suitable for walking on land.

on sand, mud, or grass. The shells of most tortoises are tall and round, while the shells of many other turtles are flat to help them glide through water. Most tortoises eat plants.

Turtles don't watch over their eggs before they hatch. Female turtles dig holes in the mud or sand. They lay their eggs in the holes, then cover up the eggs and go away. The warm sun hatches the eggs, and the babies dig their own way out.

This hawksbill turtle is about to catch a fish for lunch. The turtle's legs act like flippers, perfect for swimming.

KNOW It All! Turtles are among the world's most **endangered** animals. The hawksbill sea turtle is in danger because its beautiful tortoise shell is used to make gifts. This animal is found near tropical reefs. Many countries have passed laws against the sale of hawksbill shells. Another endangered creature is the greenish-yellow Egyptian tortoise. The tortoise, which grows to about 5 feet (1.5 meters) long, is found in Egypt, Israel, and Libya. It is a favorite among people who collect exotic, or unusual, pets.

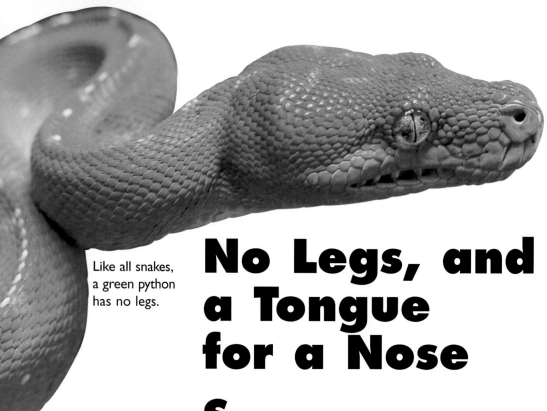

Like all snakes, a green python has no legs.

No Legs, and a Tongue for a Nose

This African egg-eating snake has no problem swallowing an egg whole.

Snakes have no legs at all, but they move very well without them! A snake can zigzag over the ground just about as fast as most people can walk.

Snakes are different from lizards because they have no ears and no eyelids. And to smell, a snake flicks out its tongue! Snakes use their good sense of smell to find their food.

Most snakes like their food alive. They eat many kinds of small animals—even other snakes. Snakes don't chew their food—they swallow it whole. Their jaws are hinged like a pair of nutcrackers. For a great big mouthful, they can release the hinges and open their mouths very wide.

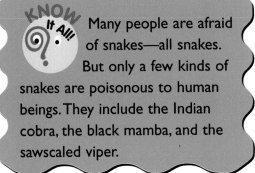

KNOW It All!! Many people are afraid of snakes—all snakes. But only a few kinds of snakes are poisonous to human beings. They include the Indian cobra, the black mamba, and the sawscaled viper.

In fact, a little garden snake can swallow a whole frog! The African egg-eating snake can swallow an egg bigger than its own head. And a big python can swallow a whole hog, hooves and all!

Pythons curl themselves around their **prey** and squeeze it to death. Other snakes, such as vipers and rattlesnakes, have poison glands. Hollow teeth, or fangs, inject the poison into the victim's body. Some kinds of cobras squirt poison at an attacker's eye.

The sea snake has a flat-sided body that paddles from side to side in the water.

A snake's tongue helps it smell things.

Ears and Eyelids

A glass snake is really a lizard. If an enemy grabs its tail, the glass snake just breaks off its tail and crawls away. This doesn't hurt the lizard a bit. It soon grows a new tail.

Sometimes it is hard to tell whether an animal is a lizard or not. Some lizards look like snakes, and some look a lot like worms.

There are three things that all lizards have. They all have eyelids that close, ears on their heads, and long tails. Most lizards also have four legs. But a few lizards, such as glass snakes and slow worms, have no legs at all.

Lizards are reptiles that live on the ground or in trees. Most live in warm, tropical regions, but some live in areas with cold winters. A lizard's scaly skin helps keep moisture inside its body even when the weather is very hot.

Unlike snakes, most lizards have four legs.

This skink emerges from leaf litter, which helps protect it from the hot Venezuelan sun.

Like other reptiles, lizards are cold-blooded. But like some **warm-blooded** animals, some lizards hibernate, or sleep through the cold winter months.

All lizards, such as the gecko, have eyelids that open and close.

This Tokay gecko lizard is shedding its skin in bits and pieces.

Growing Too Fast for Their Skin

A garter snake wiggles through the grass. Its skin has dried up and a new skin has formed beneath it. So the snake rubs its mouth against a tree trunk. The skin around its lips splits and opens up.

But this doesn't hurt the snake. Now its wrinkled old skin hangs from the tip of its tail.

Soon the snake comes to some rocks. With a twist of its tail, the snake crawls on, but the old skin stays behind. Away crawls the snake in the shiny new skin that grew beneath the old one.

Every few months a snake grows too big for its skin. Each time, it gets rid of its old skin by crawling right out of it.

Lizards cast off their skin, too. Because of their legs, however, they can't get their old skin off in one piece the way a snake can. Lizards tear off their old skins in bits and pieces.

This pilot black snake is crawling out of its old skin. Its new skin is very shiny.

Ferocious Reptiles

alligator

crocodile

Along the shore of a swamp, Spanish moss hangs down from a baldcypress tree. A turtle swims among the water lilies on the still water. But two beady eyes watch quietly nearby. Snap! The turtle has just become lunch for a hungry alligator.

Crocodiles, alligators, and caymans (KAY muhns) are large reptiles that belong to the crocodile family. They are living relatives of the dinosaurs. Scientists study them to find out what life was like long ago.

Crocodiles and alligators live in tropical places. They sun themselves along rivers and lakes or in other shallow water. Crocodiles and alligators have thicker and heavier bodies than lizards. They have long snouts with strong jaws and lots of sharp teeth.

Small crocodiles eat fish, but bigger ones can eat quite large animals, including turtles. A full-grown crocodile can kill a human being with one lash of its tail!

Most crocodiles have a snout that comes to a point in front, but an alligator's snout is rounded.

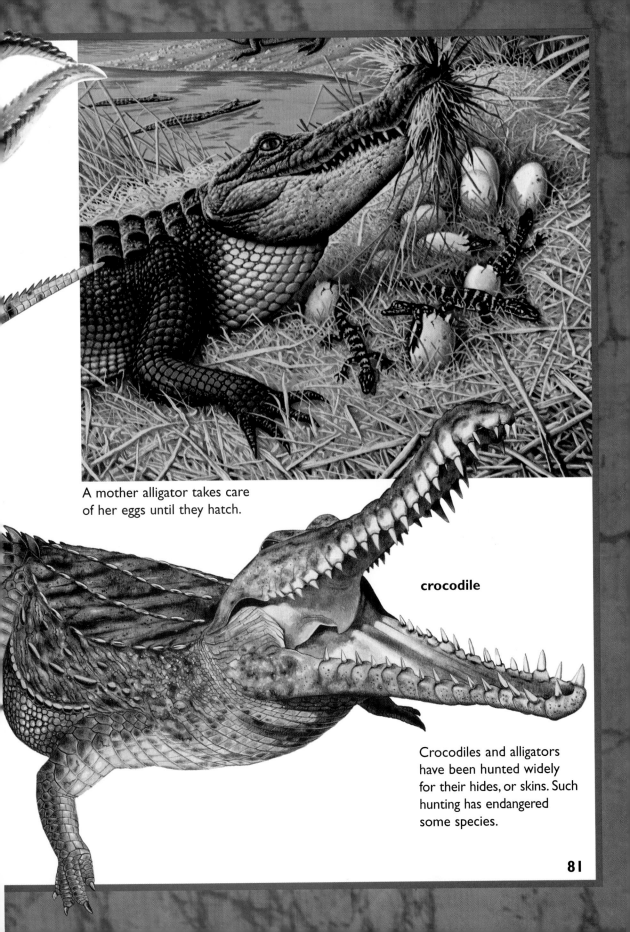

A mother alligator takes care
of her eggs until they hatch.

crocodile

Crocodiles and alligators
have been hunted widely
for their hides, or skins. Such
hunting has endangered
some species.

toad

common newts

frog

What Is an Amphibian?

Can you think of an animal that lives in the water when it is a baby and on land when it grows up? A frog! Right!

Frogs belong to a group of animals called **amphibians.** Like reptiles, amphibians are cold-blooded. But unlike reptiles, an amphibian lays eggs that are soft and have no shells. These eggs dry up easily, so amphibians must lay them in water or wet places. Most baby amphibians are born in the water. They look like baby fish, and they breathe with gills like a fish.

When most amphibians grow up, their gills disappear. Then the amphibians come on land to live. They breathe with lungs as birds, dogs, and people do.

If it is cold-blooded, and lives the first part of its life in the water and the second part on land, it's an amphibian.

spotted
salamander

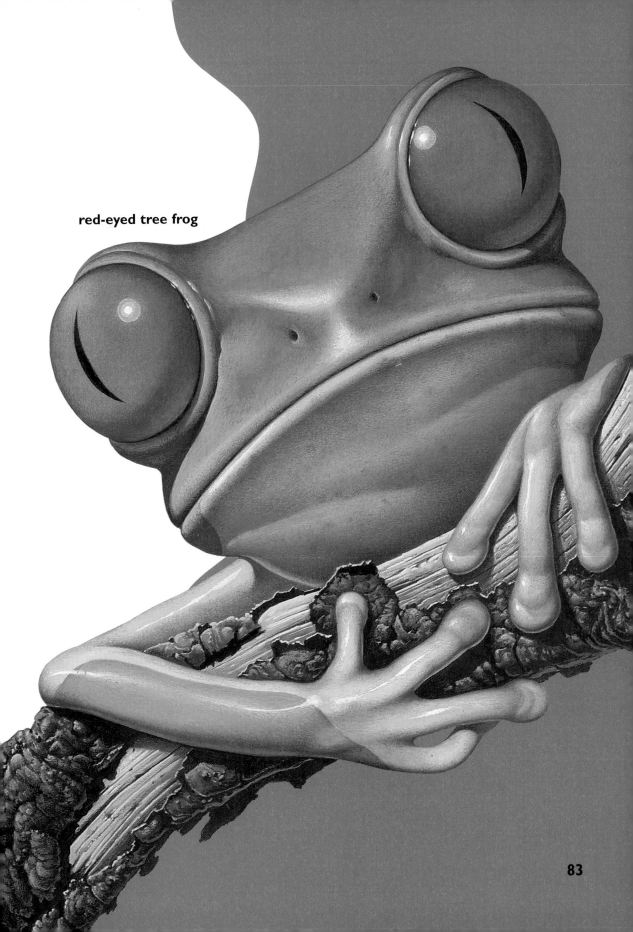

red-eyed tree frog

83

This American toad will swallow the entire earthworm, which was longer than the toad.

Amphibian Hunters

How are frogs and toads like lions and tigers? They hunt for living things to eat. But these amphibians use the tongue, not sharp claws and teeth, to catch food. Frogs and toads eat **insects** and worms— and smaller frogs and toads, too. Big bullfrogs will eat small turtles, snakes, mice, and birds.

Frogs and toads eat only things that move. An insect might be safe right in front of a frog or toad if it didn't move.

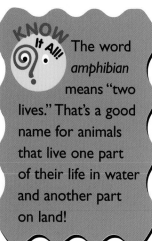

KNOW It All! The word *amphibian* means "two lives." That's a good name for animals that live one part of their life in water and another part on land!

But if the insect makes even the tiniest wiggle, the frog or toad will see it and gulp it down.

Many kinds of amphibians, including frogs and toads, use their long, sticky tongues to catch food. If an insect comes near it, the amphibian will slowly move closer and closer until—snap! Its tongue shoots out and pulls the insect into its mouth.

arrow poison frog

Some frogs are among the most poisonous animals. The brightly colored arrow poison frog of the Amazon is only about 1 inch (2.5 centimeters) long, but its skin is deadly to predators.

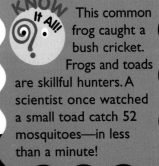

KNOW It All! This common frog caught a bush cricket. Frogs and toads are skillful hunters. A scientist once watched a small toad catch 52 mosquitoes—in less than a minute!

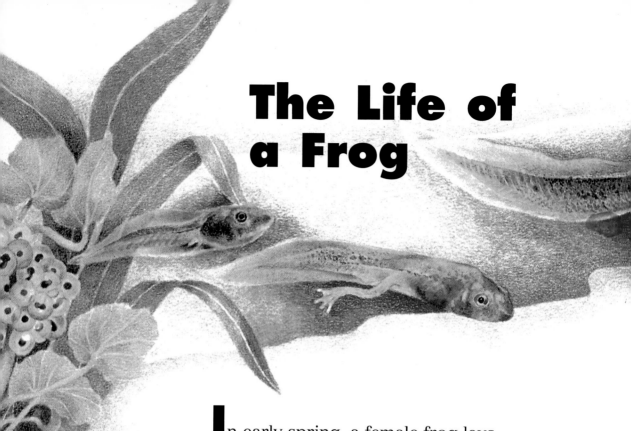

The Life of a Frog

The life cycle of many frogs takes the animal from egg to tadpole to frog in a matter of months. Do you see all the different stages in the picture above?

In early spring, a female frog lays thousands of eggs in a lake or pond. A few days or even a few weeks later, tiny wiggly tadpoles come out of the eggs.

The tadpoles swim about, nibbling at plants. They still breathe with **gills**, like fish. But lungs for breathing air are growing in their bodies.

In time, the tadpoles grow little legs. Many tadpoles are eaten by fish and water insects.

After several months, the tadpoles can leave the water and breathe air with their lungs. They are now young frogs. Their short, tadpole tails shrink away and vanish.

By summer's end, the frogs are fully grown. During winter they will hibernate at the bottom of the pond. In the spring, the females will lay new eggs.

TRY THIS!
1

An animal goes through stages from the time it is a tiny egg until the time it is a full-grown adult. These stages are part of its life cycle. Can you put these pictures of a frog's life cycle in order?

tadpoles with legs

full-grown frog

tadpoles without legs

thousands of eggs

Answers: eggs, tadpoles without legs, tadpoles with legs, full-grown frog.

Amphibians with and without Tails

This red salamander has a tail. All salamanders do.

Frogs and toads look much alike. But take a close look, and you'll see some differences. Toads are fatter than frogs and have shorter back legs. A toad's skin is rough and dry. A frog's skin is smooth and moist. Most toads have bumps on their skin that look like warts. But you won't catch warts if you touch a toad.

Frogs and toads have no tails. The amphibians called salamanders and newts all have tails. There are many kinds of newts and

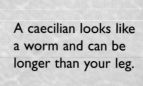

A caecilian looks like a worm and can be longer than your leg.

salamanders. Pygmy salamanders, which live in the United States, are no longer than one of your fingers. Giant salamanders live in Japan and are longer than you are tall.

mud puppy salamander

Some of the strangest of all the amphibians are the caecilians (say SIHL ee uhnz). Caecilians live in tropical lands, and they look like big, fat worms. Sometimes they are as big around as a person's thumb and as long as a person's leg—or longer!

Is it a frog or a toad? The warts and dry skin on the animal on the left tell you it is a toad. The wet skin and long back legs tell you the animal on the right is a frog.

Meet the Fish

sea horse

Dolphins and sea horses live in water. A dolphin looks like a **fish**, but it isn't. A sea horse doesn't look like a fish. But it is.

perch

How can you tell if an animal is a fish? All fish have a backbone, and all fish have **gills**. Gills are openings on a fish's head that are used for breathing.

moray eel

Most fish are covered in scales. Scales are little round or diamond-shaped pieces of hard skin.

And nearly every fish has fins on its belly, on its back or sides, or as part of its tail.

If it has gills, scales, and fins and lives in the water, it's a fish!

triggerfish

Fish-Watching

An angelfish swims in an aquarium. Its mouth opens and shuts, opens and shuts. This is how it breathes. Water goes in through its mouth and out through the gills at each side of its head. The gills take oxygen from the water, and the oxygen passes into the fish's blood. Like all animals, a fish needs oxygen to live.

As the angelfish swims, it moves its tail from side to side. This helps it to move forward. The fish uses its fins to swim, steer, and keep its balance. An air bag called a bladder helps keep it upright.

The angelfish seems to stare at you with wide eyes. Most fish have very good eyesight. With an eye on each side of its head, a fish can see in almost all directions at the same time.

The aquarium is kept in a place that is not too hot or too cold. The angelfish, like all fish, is **cold-blooded.** Its body is as warm or cold as the water around it. If the aquarium were in a cold place, the water would get too cold and the fish would die.

gills

angelfish

93

Living in Schools

At the beach, some tiny brown minnows swim near your legs. They come closer and closer and then they turn, all at once. If just one fish senses danger, it darts away. Then the fish next to it turns in a flash. The fish copy each other so quickly that they seem to be moving at the same time.

Some kinds of fish swim in groups called schools or shoals. There might be thousands of fish in the school, but they act as one. They all swim the same way, at the same speed. Fish swim in schools to stay safe. One fish swimming alone is an easy meal for a bigger creature or an easy target for somebody's fishing net. But a large group can confuse an enemy.

It is also easier for fish in schools to find food, because thousands of pairs of eyes are on the lookout. If one fish spots food and turns toward it, the whole school follows.

Not all fish live in schools. Fish that hunt **prey**, such as sharks, usually live by themselves. Other fish form schools only when they eat, rest, or lay eggs, or when they are young.

a school
of grunts

KNOW It All! A school may have many fish or just a few. For example, a school of tuna might contain 25 fish, but a school of herring may have millions!

Fish as Fish Food

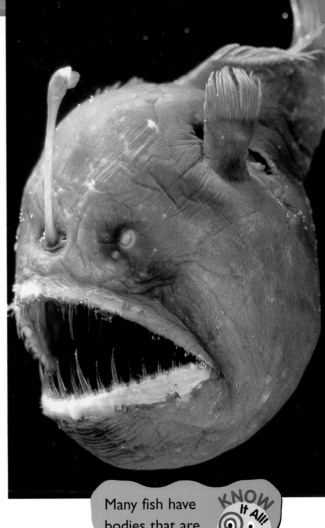

If an animal or plant lives in the water, chances are it is food for a hungry fish.

In the ocean, most fish eat only other fish. Large ocean fish, such as cod, hake, tarpon, and tuna, dine on smaller fish—herrings, sardines, and anchovies. Of course, sometimes the bigger fish are food in turn for sharks!

In rivers and lakes, fish eat fish, too. But some add other tasty things to their diet. Trout jump out of the water to snap at flying **insects**. Big hungry bass, pike, and bowfins gobble up frogs, baby ducks, and even baby muskrats.

Some kinds of fish eat plants. Carp and suckermouth catfish swim along the bottom of rivers and ponds. With tiny teeth, they chew up bits of plants that grow in the mud.

KNOW It All!

Many fish have bodies that are specially adapted for catching food. Certain fish in the deepest ocean have shiny parts that they flash to attract prey. On some anglerfish, *above*, a dangly part near the front of the body can be used as bait to catch other fish. Electric eels stun their prey with an electric shock.

brook trout

northern pike

largemouth black bass

carp

Some fish eat plants, animals, and other **organisms**. Parrotfish eat plantlike organisms called algae (AL jee) and tiny worms that live in coral. The ocean sunfish eats small shrimp, baby fish, jellyfish, and algae.

And the largest fish of all eat the smallest food. Whale sharks, giant manta rays, and basking sharks eat only **plankton**.

A worm is a tasty meal for a pumpkinseed sunfish.

Fish Fathers on Duty

Sea horses have an unusual way to care for their young. The female lays her eggs inside a pouch in the male's stomach. When the eggs hatch, the baby sea horses shoot out of the pouch, as in the photo above.

Most fish eggs never hatch. Many wash ashore and dry up, and many are eaten by other fish. So, in the dangerous world of the sea, some male fish give their eggs extra care.

A male smallmouth black bass cares for its young even before they're hatched. He makes a wide, saucer-shaped hole in the sand where the female bass lays her eggs. The eggs are sticky. They stick to the sand and do not float away.

After the female lays the eggs, the male guards them all by himself. He also fans them with his tail. This keeps the water around the eggs fresh and helps them hatch.

When the young hatch, the male watches over them as they learn to swim. He fights anything that comes near. Later, the male guards them while they find food.

A male jawfish keeps eggs in his mouth. After they hatch, he holds the young in his mouth until they're big enough to live on their own. Then he spits them out into the water, and away they swim.

This male jawfish protects eggs in his mouth as he hides in his burrow.

spotted grouper

Grunt, Croak, Squeak, and Burp

Grunt, croak, snore, squeak, click, and roar— the ocean is a noisy place! Many of these sounds are made by fish.

Most toadfish make grunting or toadlike noises.

Some fish are named for the sound they make. One kind of fish rubs its teeth together to make a grunting noise. That fish is called a grunt. Another fish is called a croaker. Can you guess why?

Pollock, haddock, angelfish, grouper, and many other fish also make grunting noises.

They grunt by vibrating some of the muscles against the swim bladder, an air-filled sac inside their bodies. The sea horse makes a clicking noise by hitting a bone on its head against a bone on its back.

angelfish

Sharks sometimes make a roaring sound. But they aren't really roaring— they're burping! Many sharks swallow air to help them stay close to the surface. When they want to dive deeper in the water, they have to burp up the air. The burp sounds like a roar.

Scientists study fish sounds to see if they mean anything. They say that many sounds seem to be made by male fish calling to female fish. Others are made by fish getting ready to fight.

When sharks burp, they sometimes make a sound like a roar.

A Wonderful, Watery World

Keeping fish as pets is fun. Many people with aquariums, or fish tanks, enjoy having fish because they come in so many shapes and sizes. The easiest fish to care for are freshwater fish, such as goldfish and guppies. Why not start your own aquarium?

You Will Need:

a 10- or 20-gallon (40- or 80-liter) glass tank

air pump and filter

clean silver sand

clean gravel

an old plate

pondweed or aquarium plants

tap water

fish food

fish

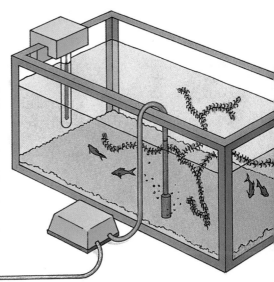

What to Do:

1. Clean the aquarium with warm water. Never use soap in the tank or to clean the sand and gravel. It will poison your fish. Put a layer of silver sand on the bottom of the tank. Cover this with gravel. Plant pondweed or aquarium plants firmly in the sand.

2. Attach a water filter and air pump to your tank. They will help keep the water fresh and clean. Then, place an old plate on the gravel, not on the plants. Pour water slowly over the plate to keep the sand and gravel from scattering. When the tank is full of water, take out the plate. Tap water is often treated with the chemical chlorine. To get rid of the chlorine, let the water sit for a few days.

3. Pick your fish. Ask your pet shop owner how many can live in your tank. Before putting the fish into the aquarium, make sure the water they are going into is the same temperature as the water they came from. Put the aquarium in a well-lit place, but not in direct sunlight. An aquarium thermometer will help you track the temperature. An aquarium cover keeps the heat—and the fish—in the tank.

4. Feed your fish small amounts of food every day. Do not overfeed them. Uneaten food sinks to the bottom of the tank and decays. This produces bacteria that can harm or even kill the fish.

5. Your tank may need cleaning as often as every one or two weeks. Ask an adult to drain about one-third of the water using a siphon hose. The hose also can be used to vacuum dirt from the gravel. Use a scraper to remove algae from the walls. Wipe the part of the glass above the water with a damp sponge. Never use soap. Refill the tank using tap water that you have let sit in an uncovered container for a few days.

With proper care, your fish should provide hours of fun.

Sharks, the Fearsome Fish

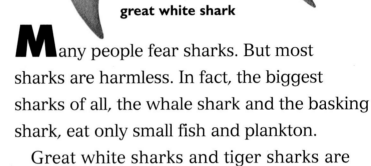

great white shark

Many people fear sharks. But most sharks are harmless. In fact, the biggest sharks of all, the whale shark and the basking shark, eat only small fish and plankton.

Great white sharks and tiger sharks are more dangerous. They eat almost anything, from garbage to big fish, seals, and sea turtles.

Small fish follow a tiger shark. They eat the leftovers after a meal.

Another dangerous shark is the hammerhead. It has a wide head shaped like a hammer, with an eye at each end. These sharks have been known to attack people.

Sharks are different from most other fish in several ways. Their skeletons are made of a tough, rubbery substance called cartilage (KAHR tuh lihdj), not bone. And the scales of sharks are not smooth like those of other fish. They are like millions of tiny, rough teeth that protect the animal. Shark's gills are open, not covered like those of other fish. They look like slits on each side of the shark's body. Sharks don't have an air bladder like other fish, either. Instead, their livers are filled with oil, which is lighter than water. Also, gulping air helps them stay afloat. Even so, if a shark stops swimming, it will sink!

whale shark

basking shark

white shark

tiger shark

thresher shark

hammerhead shark

sleeper shark

wobbegong shark

KNOW It All!!

There are about 350 species, or kinds, of sharks. Only 50 of those species are thought to be dangerous to people. Fewer than 100 shark attacks take place worldwide each year.

whale shark

Fantastic Fish

There are thousands of kinds of fish. If you tried to choose the most fantastic fish, you'd have a hard time.

The mudskipper has a head like a frog and a body like a fish. It often crawls onto land. It can jump up and catch flying insects in its mouth.

The archerfish shoots its food down with water. The archerfish swims at the top of the water until a beetle comes buzzing past. Then the fish shoots a stream of water from its mouth. The water hits the beetle with such force that it falls down into the water. The archerfish gobbles it up.

The elephant-nose mormyrid is well named. Its long nose looks like an elephant's trunk.

Leafy sea dragons are odd-looking, too. Their spiky fins make them look like pieces of seaweed.

elephant-nose mormyrid

gulper eel

an archerfish shooting water at its prey

leafy sea dragon

A gulper eel looks just like a huge mouth with a long, tapering tail attached to it. It can open its mouth wide enough to swallow a fish much larger than itself.

A flounder has both eyes on one side of its body. And let's not forget the glass catfish. You can see its insides.

These are just a few of the strange fish that live in the world. Which do you think is the most fantastic?

Meet the Invertebrates

Fish, **mammals,** and **birds** all have something in common— a backbone. They belong to a group of animals called **vertebrates**. But some of the most fantastic creatures in the sea are animals that have no backbones. They belong to a group of animals called **invertebrates**.

hermit crab

coral

Some invertebrates are huge, like the giant squid. Others are so tiny that you need a microscope to see them.

Some invertebrates, like crabs, clams, and sea spiders, have hard shells. The shells protect their soft bodies. Other invertebrates, like starfish or sea urchins, have spikes to protect them. Jellyfish and other invertebrates are soft all over. Jellyfish look like see-through blobs. They float gracefully through the sea. Their stinging tentacles are their protection!

Whether they have shells, spines, or stinging tentacles, invertebrates are some of the most interesting creatures in the sea!

octopus

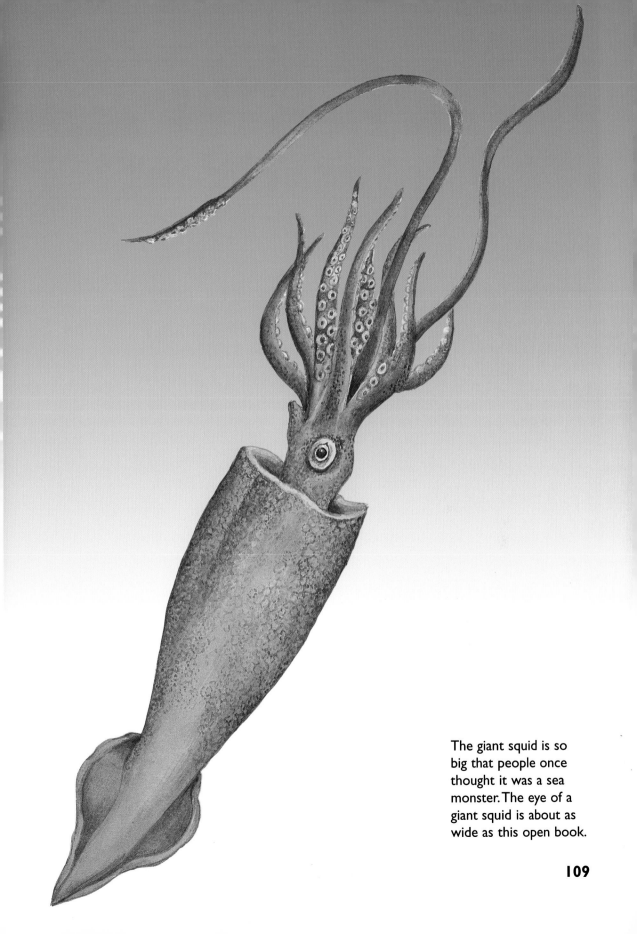

The giant squid is so big that people once thought it was a sea monster. The eye of a giant squid is about as wide as this open book.

109

sea slug

Magnificent Mollusks

Imagine having a soft body, with no backbone to hold you up and only one foot to help you move. That's what clams are like. Clams belong to a group of animals called **mollusks**. Mollusks have soft bodies with no skeleton. Some mollusks such as snails, clams, oysters, and scallops, have outer shells for protection. Slugs, octopuses, and squids are mollusks that have no outer shells.

Mollusks live in most parts of the world. Land snails and slugs live on land.

The land snail is a mollusk with a shell to protect its soft body.

Octopuses, squids, and oysters, live in the seas and oceans. Some clams and snails live in rivers, lakes, ponds, and streams.

Wherever mollusks live, they must keep their bodies moist to stay alive. That's why slugs and some land snails can be found under damp leaves or in the soil.

The giant clam lives between two shells. It can open and close its shells.

Some mollusks live between two shells that can open and close like a book. These animals are called bivalves (BY valvz). Clams, cockles, mussels, oysters, and scallops are bivalves. Bivalves usually keep their shells open just a little so that food can drift in. They eat tiny plants that float by in the water.

Mmmmmm mollusks! All around the world, people eat mollusks every day. In France, people love to eat escargot, or snails. In Italy, fried calamari, or squid, is a favorite snack. Japanese people enjoy eating giant clams. In the United States, people love to eat scallops and thick-shelled clams called quahogs.

KNOW It All!

scallop

The long, rubbery legs and staring eyes of the octopus make it a fearsome sight.

A Real Live Sea Monster

It has eight long, rubbery legs and two huge, staring eyes. The octopus is so scary-looking to some people that it is sometimes called the devilfish. But octopuses rarely attack people. They use

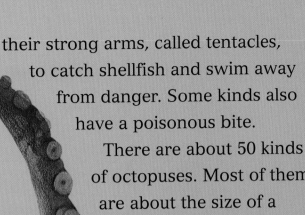

their strong arms, called tentacles, to catch shellfish and swim away from danger. Some kinds also have a poisonous bite.

There are about 50 kinds of octopuses. Most of them are about the size of a softball. But some measure 28 feet (8.5 meters) from arm tip to arm tip.

The octopus is a mollusk. It has no bones, but a tough covering called a mantle protects its body and gives it shape. Rows of round muscles under each arm act as suction cups. These suckers can hold onto an object even if the octopus's arm is cut off!

When an octopus is frightened it produces a cloud of inky liquid. The inky liquid makes it hard for an enemy to see or smell the octopus. That's how the octopus gets away.

The word *octopus* comes from a Greek word that means "eight feet."

KNOW It All!

An Underwater Flower Garden

A spider crab feeds on the soft polyps of living coral.

An animal that looks like a tiny flower floats down through the sea. It fastens itself to the sandy sea floor. Then it takes chemicals out of the water and builds a tiny stone cup around itself.

Soon the little animal buds, just as a flower does. The bud grows and becomes another flower animal. The new animal builds a stone cup around itself and then it buds too.

The tiny stone cups build up year after year, layer upon layer. And inside each cup is a little flowerlike animal.

The flowerlike animals inside are called polyps (PAH luhps). Polyps are colored red, pink, orange, blue, green, or purple. At night, they stretch and hold out arms that look like flower petals. The arms catch tiny animals that float in the water.

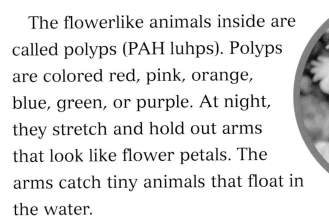

closeup of coral polyps

All the stone cups stuck together are called coral. Coral may be shaped like a bush, a fan, a round ball, or a bunch of lace. When a polyp is open inside each cup, the coral looks like a field of flowers.

Many colorful creatures live and hide in the crevices and tunnels created by coral.

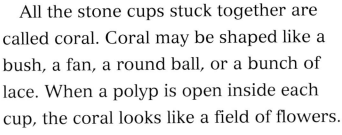

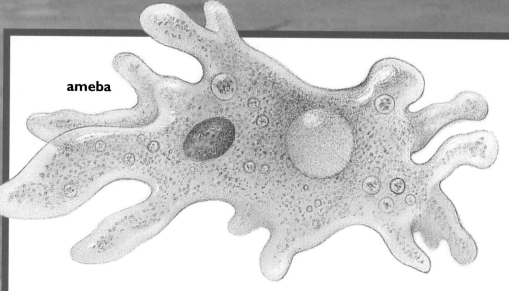

ameba

Life Under a Microscope

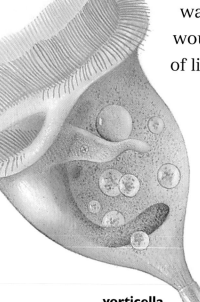

vorticella

If you picked up a cupful of seawater, you might see a few creatures. But, if you looked at the same cup of water under a microscope, you would see hundreds or thousands of little creatures!

Some of the creatures are like tiny animals. Some are the babies of bigger animals. You'd also see living things like plants. Huge masses of these animals and plants drift in the ocean. Together they are called **plankton**. Plankton is food for a great many sea creatures, from shrimp to whales.

In a cupful of pond water you would see different creatures. One looks like the bottom of a shoe. It's called a paramecium (PAIR uh MEE shee uhm) and has no head and no legs. It doesn't have eyes or a mouth either. Its body is covered with rows of little hairs that it uses like oars to move through the water.

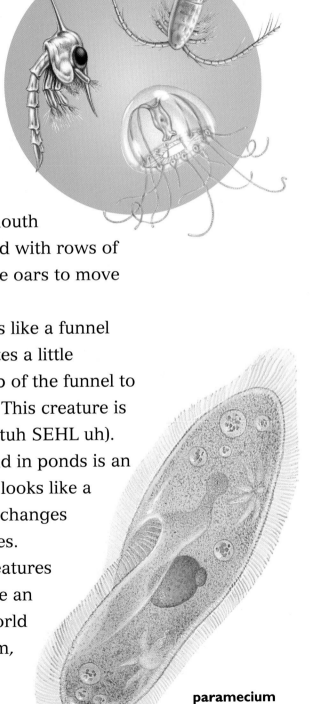

plankton

Another creature looks like a funnel with a long tube. It creates a little whirlpool around the top of the funnel to draw food into its body. This creature is called a vorticella (VAWR tuh SEHL uh).

Another creature found in ponds is an ameba (uh MEE buh). It looks like a blob of gray jelly, and it changes shape every time it moves.

Even though these creatures are microscopic, they are an important part of the world of animals. Without them, many other animals would go hungry.

paramecium

A starfish pulls a clam's shell apart. Then the starfish puts its stomach into the shell and digests the clam.

Starry Creatures

What kind of animal has eyes and feet on its arms and pushes its stomach out of its body when it eats? A starfish!

Starfish have tough-skinned bodies shaped like a star. They usually have five arms, sometimes more. Underneath each arm there are little tubes. These are the feet of the starfish. And the small reddish spots at the end of each arm are its eyes!

When it finds a clam, the starfish climbs on top of it. Its tube feet stick to the clamshell like glue. Then the starfish slowly begins to pull the shell apart. Soon the shell is a little way open—just a tiny crack. The starfish then pushes its stomach through an opening in its body and between the two halves of the shell. Juices from the starfish's stomach turn the clam to mush. The starfish digests, or breaks down, the clam inside the clam's own shell.

If a starfish loses an arm, it grows a new one! In fact, if the starfish is torn in two, each half grows into a new starfish.

sea cucumber

Fuzzy Cookies and More

sand dollar

The ocean is full of amazing animals. A sand dollar looks like a fuzzy cookie, but it's an animal that lives in the sand. It moves about on many feet that look like tiny tubes. People often find the white coin-shaped skeletons of sand dollars on the beach.

A sea cucumber isn't found in a garden. It's an animal with a long round body that looks a little like a garden cucumber. At one end are its "fingers" and mouth. The animal uses its fingers to catch food floating in the water. Then it puts each finger, one at a time, into its mouth and enjoys a tasty meal.

Another unusual animal looks like a creeping pincushion. This creature, called a sea urchin, is related to the starfish, but it is round and plump.

This sea urchin looks like a pincushion. Its spines help protect it from enemies.

Sea peaches belong to the family of animals called sea squirts. Most kinds of sea squirts are just round bodies with two openings like little mouths. One mouth sucks water in. The other squirts water out. The sea squirt eats the tiny animals and bits of plants in the water it sucks in.

A sea peach sucks in water, then squirts it out!

121

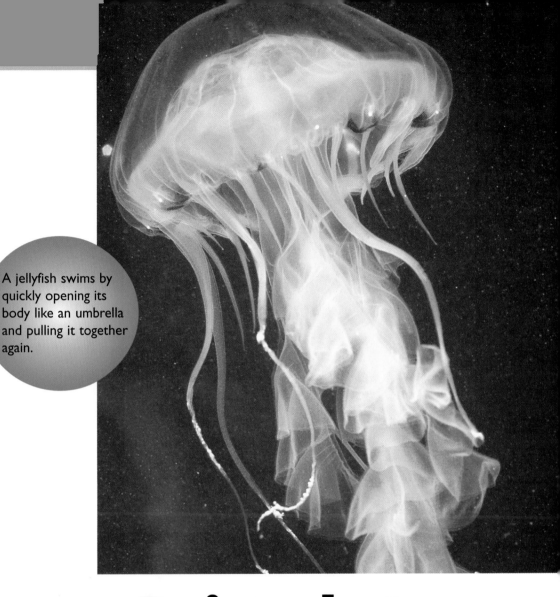

A jellyfish swims by quickly opening its body like an umbrella and pulling it together again.

Dainty but Deadly

Some of the daintiest creatures in the sea are the deadliest to small fish and shrimp. Both the sea anemone (uh NEHM uh nee) and the jellyfish look like pretty flowers, but they sting their **prey** with poison.

The sea anemone got its name because it looks like the flower called an anemone. The animal lives on the bottom of the sea, often in a warm coral reef or a rock pool. A sea anemone can move slowly, but it prefers to stay in one spot.

To catch small fish and shrimp to eat, the sea anemone spreads out its arms. Those arms are filled with tiny stinging parts. When the anemone touches its prey, it shoots out a poison. The poison stops the creature from moving. Then the sea anemone uses its arms to carry the creature to its mouth.

The jellyfish looks like an upside-down tulip. Its body is like a see-through umbrella with long strings hanging down. The jellyfish is made mostly of water. Washed up on the beach, it looks like a lump of colorless jelly.

The jellyfish swims by opening and closing its whole body. When it stops moving, it sinks to the bottom. As it drifts down, it catches small animals by stinging them with its tentacles.

sea anemone

Meet the Arthropods

ladybug

What's an eight-legged creature that catches other animals in a trap? A spider! What six-legged jumping animal has ears on its sides? A grasshopper! What's a ten-legged tunnel builder? A crayfish, or crawfish!

The world is full of these many-legged creatures called **arthropods** (AHR thruh pahdz). An arthropod's body is divided into several sections. Each section is covered with an outer shell. Arthropods have no skeleton inside their bodies, but their hard shell protects them. Large arthropods, such as lobsters, have a thick, heavy shell. Small, flying arthropods like bees have a much lighter covering.

crayfish

wolf spider

Arthropods live everywhere—jungles, deserts, oceans, caves, mountaintops, and in your own backyard. You can watch them creep, crawl, and fly all summer long.

If it has many legs and its body is divided into several sections, it's an arthropod.

grasshopper

Creeping on Six Legs

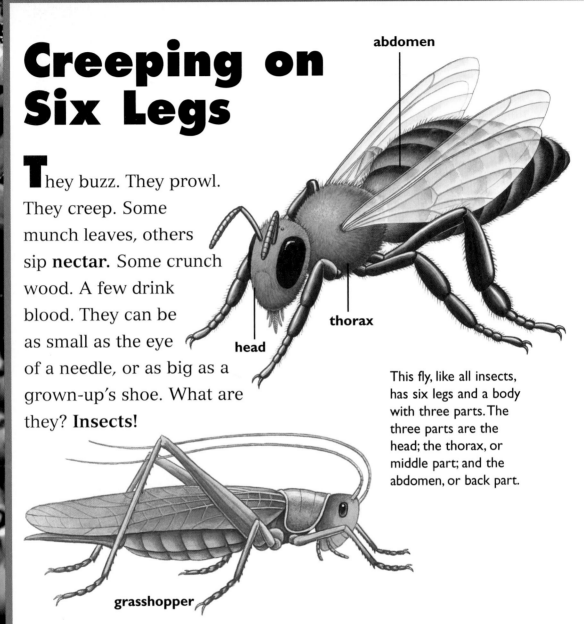

abdomen

head

thorax

grasshopper

They buzz. They prowl. They creep. Some munch leaves, others sip **nectar.** Some crunch wood. A few drink blood. They can be as small as the eye of a needle, or as big as a grown-up's shoe. What are they? **Insects!**

This fly, like all insects, has six legs and a body with three parts. The three parts are the head; the thorax, or middle part; and the abdomen, or back part.

Insects live just about everywhere, from the steamiest jungles to the coldest mountaintops and the driest deserts. No matter where you live, you're sure to see insects buzz, prowl, or creep by.

Flies, ants, bees, grasshoppers, beetles, crickets, and butterflies are all in the group of animals called insects. Like all insects, these creatures have six legs. Most insects also have wings.

Insects do some amazing things. Some insects, like flies, taste with their feet. Most insects smell with two

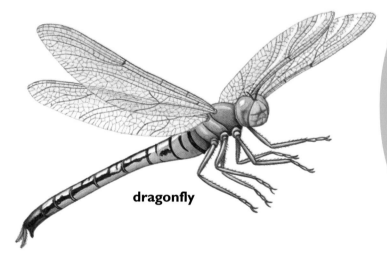

dragonfly

wiggly feelers called antennae (an TEHN ee). Some insects have no eyes, while others have five or more. Many insects hear with hairs on their bodies, while others have "ears" on their legs or on the sides of their bodies.

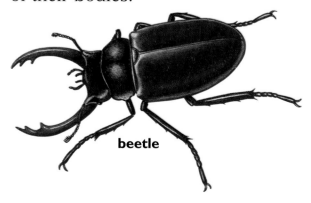

beetle

KNOW It All! Moths and butterflies are insects that look alike. Here is how you can tell the difference between the two.

- Most butterflies fly during the daytime, while most moths fly at night.

- Most butterflies have knobs at the ends of their antennae, while most moths do not.

- Most butterflies have slim, hairless bodies. The bodies of most moths are plump and furry.

- Most butterflies rest with their wings upright over their bodies. Most moths rest with their wings stretched out flat.

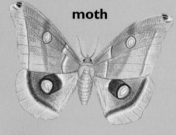

moth

butterfly

An Amazing Change

Butterflies are beautiful, but their lives are short. Most butterflies live only about a week, just long enough to find a mate. When butterflies mate and the female lays eggs, they are repeating an amazing process. The eggs change from caterpillar to adult butterfly in a process called **metamorphosis** (meht uh MOR fuh sihs).

6. About the twelfth day, the pupa cracks open and a monarch butterfly struggles out. Soon its wings flatten and spread out, and it flies away.

5. The caterpillar sheds its skin and forms a hard shell, or cocoon. The caterpillar is now a pupa or chrysalis. It hangs upside down for 12 days. Inside the shell it slowly changes shape.

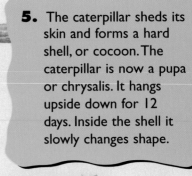

1. A monarch butterfly lays her eggs on the underside of a leaf.

2. Four days later, the eggs hatch into tiny caterpillars. Each tiny caterpillar has 16 legs and 12 eyes—6 on each side of its body.

3. The hungry caterpillar eats and eats and grows bigger and bigger. From time to time its skin splits and it grows a new one.

4. After two weeks, the caterpillar attaches itself to a twig with a sticky knob of silk.

129

Tiny but Deadly

When you think about dangerous animals, do you think of fierce sharks and hungry lions? You should also think about another dangerous animal—the common housefly. Why? Because flies carry germs, and some germs cause disease!

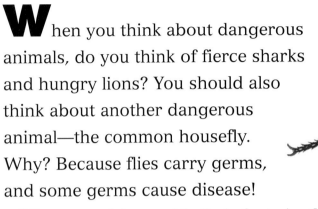

common housefly

Flies taste things with their feet. As they walk over all kinds of rotting foods and plants, they collect germs on their feet. Then they land on fresh food, leaving germs everywhere.

A female mosquito settles on a flying squirrel, ready to suck the animal's blood.

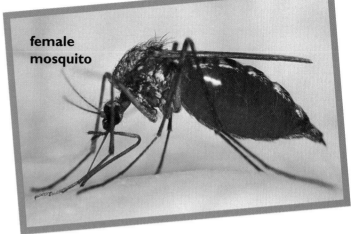

female mosquito

Flies also spread germs when they eat. A fly can eat only liquids. It pumps a special juice from its stomach that turns food into liquid. The fly might suck up food that has germs in it. This means some of the germs get into the fly's stomach. If the fly pumps some stomach juice onto the sugar on your table, the germs get into the sugar. And if you eat the sugar, the germs get into you. Yuck!

The mosquito can also be a dangerous enemy. Female mosquitoes drink people's blood! They break the skin and suck the blood with their long mouthparts, leaving an itchy bite. Sometimes, when mosquitoes drink blood, they inject tiny germs into the bloodstream. The germs mosquitoes carry can cause serious diseases.

cockroach on a cracker

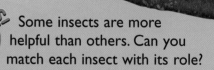

TRY THIS!

1 Some insects are more helpful than others. Can you match each insect with its role?

1. cockroach
2. mosquito
3. bee
4. boll weevil
5. ladybug

a. pollinates flowers and vegetables; makes honey
b. destroys crops
c. bites people and carries disease
d. eats harmful insects
e. eats and spoils food in homes

Answers: 1. e; 2. c; 3. a; 4. b; 5. d.

A Wood-Ant City

An ant nest is like a little city where hundreds or even thousands of ants live together. Ants make their nests by digging tunnels and storerooms in the ground. Some also build mounds above ground, and cover them with twigs.

The picture on the next page shows part of a wood-ant nest. If you look at it carefully, you can see a lot going on. Above the nest, a group of workers hunts for food. The ant with wings is a male. Male ants don't do any work.

Inside the nest, in the top tunnel, two workers are bringing in part of a leaf. They will use it to repair the nest. Other workers are getting ready to carry cocoons to another room. Inside each cocoon is a baby ant. When the babies grow up they will break out of the cocoons.

In the next tunnel is the queen ant. She is much bigger than the workers. She spends her whole life laying eggs.

Ants work as if they were quite smart, but an ant does things because its body gets signals, such as smells. Different smells make ants do different things.

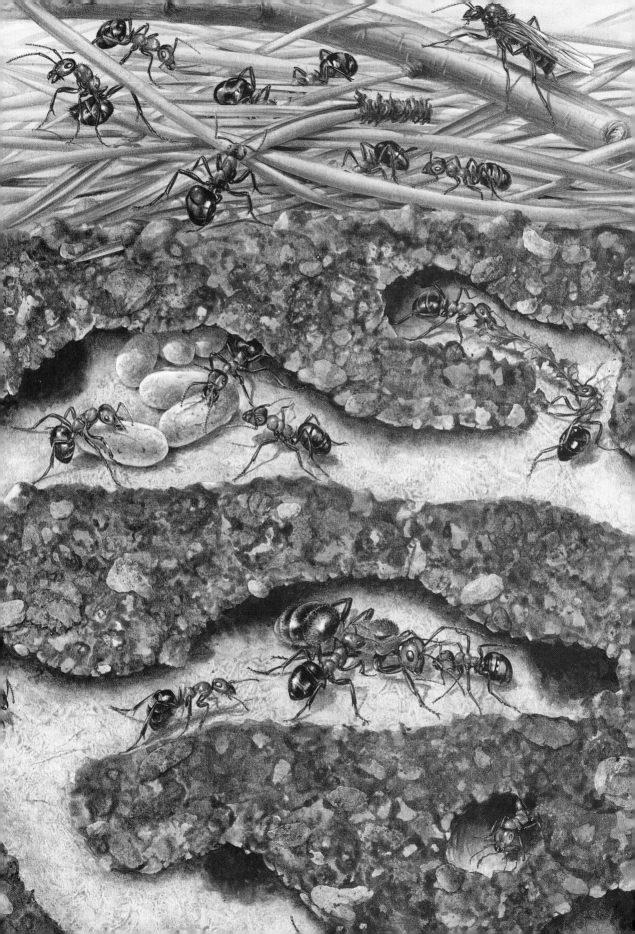

The Buzz on Bees

A honey bee lands on a flower. It stretches out its tubelike tongue and sucks up the sweet nectar. As the bee pushes into the flower, a yellow powder called **pollen** falls onto the bee's hairy body. The pollen then rubs off on every flower the bee visits after that. A flower needs pollen from another flower of the same kind to make seeds.

The inside of a bee hive has thousands of tiny rooms called cells. Some of the cells shown here are filled with honey.

Honey bees also take some pollen for themselves. They mix it with a tiny bit of nectar and carry it on their back legs. When the bee is fully loaded with nectar and pollen, it flies back to the hive. There worker bees take the nectar and pollen. In a few days the nectar will thicken to honey.

Inside the hive there are thousands of tiny rooms, or cells. The cells are storerooms. Some are filled with honey or pollen, food for the bees. Others contain eggs or bee larvae. Others hold baby bees in silky cocoons. These young bees are changing into adults.

This honey bee's legs are covered with pollen.

tarantula

Crawling on Eight Legs

Many people shudder when
they see a spider. But most
spiders are harmless,
and some are even helpful.
How do spiders help people? They
eat many harmful insects. They munch
grasshoppers and locusts, which destroy
crops. They also snap up flies and
mosquitoes, which carry disease.

Many people think spiders are
insects. But they are not. Insects have
wings, feelers, and six legs. Spiders have
neither wings nor feelers, and they have
eight legs. Eight-legged animals are
called **arachnids** (uh RAK nihdz).

yellow
garden
spider

Scorpions are close relatives of spiders. Scorpions live in warm, dry places such as deserts. Scorpions have eight legs, like spiders. But mother scorpions don't lay eggs, as many spiders do. Baby scorpions come out of the mother's body. They climb up onto her back and hang on as she carries them around.

This scorpion is drawing a victim into its mouth. Yum!

A scorpion uses its claws to grab its prey. Then it pulls the victim into its mouth and chews it up. Sometimes the scorpion kills its prey with a poisonous sting. The stinger is a sharp, curved spike at the end of the scorpion's tail. The stings of some scorpions are dangerous to people.

The Web Weavers

This fisher spider has caught its meal.

Many kinds of spiders spin webs to catch flying insects. Each kind of spider makes its own special kind of web, from small, sticky traps to large, tightly woven nets. Orb spiders make webs with threads that stretch from the center like the spokes of a bicycle wheel. Black widow spiders make tangled webs. Grass spiders make webs like little sheets.

Spiderwebs are made of silk that comes out of the spider's body. The silk is a liquid that forms a thin, strong thread when air touches it. After a spider spins its web, it hangs underneath it or hides nearby. An insect caught in the web shakes the web as it struggles, telling the spider that dinner is ready!

Some spiders have other ways to catch their food. Wolf spiders and lynx spiders chase insects. Jumping spiders catch insects by jumping on them. Some spiders even like to fish! They wait beside a stream or pond and catch water insects that swim past.

This female garden spider is waiting for a meal to get caught in her web.

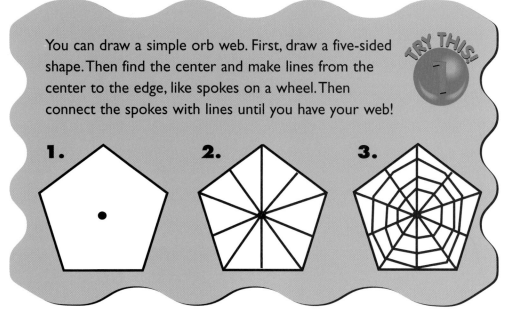

You can draw a simple orb web. First, draw a five-sided shape. Then find the center and make lines from the center to the edge, like spokes on a wheel. Then connect the spokes with lines until you have your web!

TRY THIS!

1.

2.

3.

Arthropods of the Sea

Many kinds of arthropods live in the sea. Lobsters, shrimps, crabs, and barnacles are all arthropods that live in the sea. They are called crustaceans. That means animals with crusts. Every part of a lobster's body is covered with a crust of hard skin, like armor. Crustaceans have hard shells, 10 legs, and 4 feelers, or antennae. Because they live mostly in the water, crustaceans breathe with gills, like fish.

Lobsters use eight of their ten legs for walking along the ocean floor. The other two legs are used like arms. Each arm ends in a fierce-looking pincer, or claw.

Shrimps look like tiny lobsters. Some kinds of shrimps are so small they can be seen only with a microscope.

red coral shrimp

common lobster

Crabs have flat bodies. The tail is tucked forward under the rest of the body. Instead of walking forward, crabs scuttle sideways along the seashore or in shallow rock pools.

Barnacles are crustaceans that fasten themselves to rocks or the bottoms of ships. They are closed up inside their shells, and only their legs stick out. They wiggle their legs to pull in food that floats past in the water.

goose barnacles

fiddler crabs feeding on a muddy shore

Amazing Animals

ajolote

Do you know of a mammal that lays eggs? A bright blue lizard with stubby legs? Or a fish that can walk on land? There are millions of different mammals, and some are truly fantastic.

The platypus (PLAT uh puhs) and the echidna (ih KIHD nuh) are mammals that seem to be part bird. The platypus looks like it has the body of a beaver and the bill and feet of a duck. The echidna looks like a porcupine with a pointy snout. Female platypuses and echidnas give milk, like all mammal females, but they also lay eggs, like all female birds.

walking fish

The bright blue lizard called an ajolote (ah hoh LUH tay) looks like a worm with legs. It uses its two tiny front legs to crawl and dig holes. The walking fish will drown if it stays underwater too long. It has to come to the top of the water to gulp air. Sometimes it even crawls out of the water. It pulls itself along with its fins. Turn the page to read more about amazing animals.

echidna

Inches	0	1/2	1		2		3		4		5

Centimeters

0 1 2 3 4 5 6 7 8 9 10 11 12 13

Biggest and Smallest

blue whale

blue whale

Mammals

The Kitti's hog-nosed bat is the smallest mammal. It's no bigger than a bumblebee, less than 1 inch (2.5 centimeters) long. The blue whale is the largest mammal. It's as long as five elephants in a row, or 100 of the rulers shown above. The bat and the whale are both **mammals**. So is a dog.

Kitti's
hog-nosed
bat

bee hummingbird

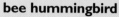

ostrich

Birds

The bee hummingbird is the smallest bird. It's no longer than one of your fingers, 2 inches (5 centimeters) long. The ostrich is the biggest bird. It's taller than a tall person, and as tall as eight of the rulers shown above. The ostrich and the bee hummingbird are **birds.** So is a sparrow.

Reptiles

The West Indian gecko is 2 inches (5 centimeters) long. One type of West Indian gecko is so small that it can take a nap in a tablespoon. The reticulate python is one of the longest reptiles. It's as long as six bicycles in a row, or 30 of the rulers. The gecko and the python are both **reptiles**. So is a turtle.

**West Indian
gecko**

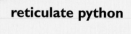
reticulate python

144

giant spider crab

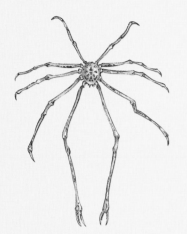

mite

Arthropods

A mite is the smallest arthropod. It is smaller than the period at the end of this sentence. The smallest mites are so tiny you can't see them without a microscope. A giant spider crab is the biggest arthropod. Its body can reach 13 feet (4 meters) across, or 13 of the rulers! The mite and the spider crab are both **arthropods**. So is an ant.

Fish

The dwarf goby is the smallest fish. It's no longer than your fingernail, about 1/2 inch (1 centimeter) long. The whale shark is the biggest fish. It's a little longer than a railroad train boxcar, or 50 of the rulers. The goby and the whale shark are both **fish.** So is a goldfish.

Amphibians

The Cuban tree frog is the smallest amphibian. It's about the size of a small coin, or about 1/2 inch (1 centimeter) long. The giant salamander is the biggest amphibian. It's about as long as a bicycle, or five of the rulers. The salamander and frog are both **amphibians**. So is a toad.

giant salamander

dwarf goby

whale shark

Cuban tree frog

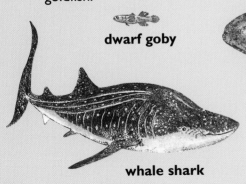

Note: *The illustrations on these pages are not drawn to scale.*

The hedgehog's short, sharp spines warn other animals to stay away.

Animal Armor

When it is scared, the porcupine fish fills its body with water to make its spines stick out.

If you saw a pangolin (payng GOH luhn) you might say it looked like a pine cone with legs and a tail.

A pangolin is one of the animals that is protected by armor. It's covered with scales like those on a pine cone, only bigger. When a pangolin is frightened, it rolls itself into a ball. Then it tucks its head between its legs and covers its stomach with its tail. Its sharp-edged scales stick up. Not even a tiger would dare to bite through it.

When a pangolin, *below*, is frightened, it rolls itself into a ball, *bottom*.

The armadillo is another animal in armor. An armadillo is born with soft skin. But as it grows, its skin becomes covered with small, flat pieces of bone. This bony armor covers much of the armadillo's body. The armadillo protects itself by rolling up into a hard, bony ball that even a wolf finds hard to bite.

Porcupines, hedgehogs, porcupine fish, and sea urchins wear a sort of armor, too. Their bodies are covered with sharp spines that keep other animals from biting them. These animals can't run fast or fight well. But wearing armor helps them stay alive.

KNOW It All!

The word *armadillo* means "little armored thing." This photo shows a nine-banded armadillo. Can you see its nine narrow bands of bony plates?

This frightened snake is pretending to be dead so that its enemy will go away.

Animal Pretenders

Sometimes, in the world of animals, it's eat or be eaten. To stay safe from **predators**, some animals hide in clever ways or pretend to be something else.

It's hard to see a green grasshopper on a leaf, a striped tiger in tall grass, or a brown lizard on the bark of a tree. Their color makes them hard to see in their **habitats**. Some **insects** are also experts at hide-and-seek. Their bodies are shaped like leaves or twigs, or even like bird droppings. These ways of blending into the background are called camouflage (CAM uh

Many animals mistake a walkingstick for a twig.

Both of these butterflies are protected by their bright colors. A monarch butterfly, *below*, tastes bad to birds. Birds are warned off by its bright colors. A viceroy butterfly, *left*, doesn't taste bad, but it looks so much like a monarch that birds leave it alone, too.

flahj). It makes the animals hard to find, so they are safe from predators.

Other animals are actors—they trick predators into leaving them alone. When the Australian frilled lizard is frightened, it unfolds a big flap of skin around its neck and opens its mouth wide. The small, harmless lizard suddenly looks big and dangerous. The opossum and the eastern hognose snake lie on their back and "play dead" when they feel threatened.

How well some animals can hide or act often decides whether they will be able to look for food—or become food themselves!

The Australian frilled lizard looks scary, but it is small and harmless.

Safety in Numbers

This herd of baboons looks relaxed, but each animal is ready to warn the others of danger if necessary.

A herd of baboons hunts for food at the edge of a grassy plain in Africa. Each baboon is looking and listening every second. There might be a lion creeping through the grass toward the herd!

If a baboon saw or heard something, it would give a loud grunt. Baboon grunts sound almost like someone yelling "Hah!" Then all the baboons would hurry to

climb trees. Because of one baboon's
warning, all the baboons would be safe.

Some animals live together in herds.
They are safer that way. An animal by
itself may not see or hear the enemy that
creeps toward it. But if there are many
animals watching, there are many more
chances that one animal will see or smell
danger and warn the others.

Herds of baboons, zebras, antelopes,
and deer run when they sense danger.
But sometimes a whole herd of animals
will fight an enemy.

Sometimes the safest place to be is in
a herd. There is safety in numbers!

Song and Dance

This frog is preparing to croak loudly.

Have you ever seen fireflies flashing on a summer night? If so, you've seen male fireflies looking for mates. The male firefly flashes his light to attract a female. Animals use all sorts of things— light, colorful feathers, and even food—to attract mates.

The male satin bowerbird of Australia builds a kind of house out of grass and twigs. It decorates the house with bright stones, flowers, and seeds. When a female comes near, the male spreads its wings and "dances."

Other animals make "songs" to attract mates. Crickets and grasshoppers make a loud sound by rubbing their wings together, or by scraping a leg against a wing. Many frogs and toads blow up a large sac under their chin. This makes their croaking sound extra loud.

Some animals use "perfume" to attract a mate. Female silkworm moths release sweet-scented chemicals to attract males.

For some females, food is a gift of love. A male tern catches a fish and offers it to the female. Male nursery-web spiders present the female with a captured fly before mating.

The female satin bowerbird sits in a fancy nest, which the male has built for her.

A grasshopper "sings" by rubbing its wings together. He hopes the sound will attract a mate.

Look out! An animal is nearby. The goose beats her wings, hisses, and honks. This frightens the animal away.

Warning!

Have you ever wondered what animals are "saying" when they tweet, squeak, mew, or bark?

Sometimes, animals make sounds to find a mate. But other sounds are calls for help or cries of danger. A dolphin that is hurt makes a high whistling noise to get the attention of other dolphins. The other dolphins use their backs and flippers to keep the injured dolphin near the top of the water so it can breathe.

Some animals "talk" without using any sounds. Deer and many other animals mark their territory by rubbing a special scent on trees or bushes. Glands in the faces of some male deer give off a scent that warns other males to stay away.

Wolves are among many animals who use special cries to communicate with each other.

Other animals communicate by changing their body positions. Whenever two wolves in the same family meet, they use their bodies to show which wolf has a higher rank, or position. The high-ranking wolf stands straight, holds its tail high, and points its ears forward. A low-ranking wolf crouches, holds its tail between its legs, and flattens its ears.

A rabbit warns other rabbits of danger by thumping the ground.

A ground squirrel whistles to others that a hawk is circling above.

Animal Partners

Hungry crocodiles usually try to eat birds that come near them. But one kind of bird can walk among crocodiles safely. In fact, this bird can lay its eggs in crocodile nests!

A bird called the water dikkop eats insects that disturb crocodiles. The bird gets an easy meal and the crocodile becomes more comfortable. So the birds are really helping the crocodiles. Maybe that's why the crocodiles don't harm them.

A wrasse cleans a moray eel.

Little fish called wrasses (RAS uhz) help many other fish. Tiny worms often fasten themselves to a fish and make sores on its body. When this happens, the fish goes to a coral reef where a wrasse lives. The little wrasse hunts all over the fish's body and eats the worms.

A European fish called a bitterling teams up with certain freshwater clams. The female bitterling lays her eggs in the clam. When the baby fish leave the shell, clam larvae are buried in their skin. After the clam larvae have grown a bit, they leave the fish and sink to the bottom of the pond or river. The clam provides a safe place for the fish to lay its eggs, and the fish helps spread baby clams along the pond bottom.

The water dikkop, the wrasse, and the bitterling all get something from the animals they help. Some get food as a reward for getting rid of pesky pests. Others help each other reproduce.

Oxpecker birds ride on the backs of black rhinoceroses. They eat the insects that bite rhinoceroses.

Sleeping Through Winter

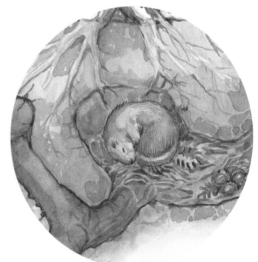

A woodchuck sleeps all winter in its underground home.

Every autumn, a woodchuck eats large amounts of food, curls up into a ball, and goes to sleep in its underground home. But the woodchuck's sleep isn't like your sleep. The woodchuck's heart and breathing slow down and nearly stop. Its body changes. Most of the time, the woodchuck's body is warm because it is a **warm-blooded** animal. But the woodchuck's body grows cold before it goes into its long winter sleep. As it sleeps, its body lives off the energy from the extra food it ate in autumn.

A water snake hibernates underground.

The woodchuck's sleep is called hibernation (HY buhr nay shun). Ground squirrels, bats, and some other warm-blooded animals also hibernate.

A swarm of ladybugs gathers in a sheltered place to hibernate.

Snakes, turtles, frogs, and toads hibernate in a different way. A snake is **cold-blooded**. Its body is just as warm or as cold as the air around it. So when the weather grows colder, a snake's body grows colder. The snake tries to get warm by crawling into a hole. But as the weather becomes colder, the snake's body becomes cold and stiff. Its heart and breathing nearly stop.

When spring comes, the woodchucks and other warm-blooded animals wake up. The snakes warm up, too, and crawl out of their holes. The world is alive again!

Caribou travel in large
herds in search of food.

Animals on the Move

When winter comes, many animals
find it hard to find food. So they fly,
march, scamper, or swim to warmer
places. When spring comes, they fly,
march, scamper, and swim back. This
movement from place to place as the
seasons change is called **migration**
(my GRAY shuhn).

Barn swallows, monarch butterflies,
ladybugs, caribou, whales, salmon, and
lemmings are just a few of the animals
that migrate.

When birds migrate, they often fly great
distances. Sometimes they cross oceans
and continents. In spring, they migrate
back. Sometimes they return to the same
nests they used the summer before.

In winter, caribou leave their summer home in northern North America and begin a dangerous journey southward in large herds. The following spring they journey northward again.

Lemmings are small mammals that live in northern Europe. They migrate sometimes, too. When there is a lot of food, lemmings have many young. When the food runs out, they migrate. Sometimes they travel along roads and through towns looking for food.

KNOW It All!

Salmon don't migrate to find food, as many other animals do. Salmon make long trips upriver from the sea to lay their eggs. Like the salmon shown here, they swim upstream, making amazing leaps out of the water to get up a waterfall. When they reach a quiet, shallow spot, they lay their eggs. This is called spawning.

Every animal is part of
nature's food chain.

Food Chain

A field of green grass waves in the wind.
A furry rabbit hops by and nibbles the
grass. As the rabbit scurries around, an owl
perches overhead. The owl swoops down,
grabs the rabbit, and flies away to eat it.
When it has eaten its fill, the owl leaves
part of the rabbit's body in another field of
grass. The rabbit's body feeds the soil.

It may seem cruel that animals kill and eat
one another. But this is just one way in
which wild creatures help each other and
keep nature in balance. The grass, the

rabbit, and the owl are part of an important system in nature called a **food chain**.

All food chains begin with sunlight. Sunlight provides food for plants. Plants are the primary **producers** in a food chain. They use sunlight, water, and air to produce food to live and grow.

Animals that eat plants are another link in the food chain. They are **consumers**. Animals that eat the plant-eating animals are also consumers. The rabbit and the owl are consumers.

Tiny living things called **decomposers** are also part of the food chain. They break down dead plants and animals into parts. These parts nourish the soil in which the plants grow.

Whenever you eat a hamburger or a piece of fish, you are part of a food chain.

Nature's Cleanup Crew

What happens to the leaves that fall from trees every autumn? Mold grows inside the leaves, making them rot. The leaves begin to fall apart. In the spring, millions of baby insects eat into the leaves.

Then earthworms, slugs, and insects go to work. They chew the leaves to pieces. The leaves are digested and pass out of their bodies as waste. Mold and tiny creatures called bacteria (bac TIHR ee uh) change the waste into gases and liquids that living plants need. Without those things, the plants would die. And without plants, animals couldn't live. By the next autumn, there's nothing left of last year's leaves.

Mold and bacteria go to work on dead animals, too. Then their bodies put nutrients, or foods, back into the soil for plants to use.

Some burying beetles, such as the sexton beetle, eat dead animals. They do something else, too. They dig underneath the body. The body slowly sinks deeper until it is completely buried. The male and female beetles are buried with it. The mother beetle lays her eggs on the body and, when the eggs hatch, the larvae eat the rest of the dead animal.

A number of animals live off dead creatures. Hyenas and vultures clean up carcasses left by lions.

Animals in Danger

The central Asian cobra is overcollected for trade.

The black rhinoceros is overhunted for its horns.

Hundreds of years ago, thousands of birds called dodos lived on the earth. But people overhunted them for food and introduced new animal enemies to their habitats. Now there are no dodo birds. Today, the numbers of polar bears, rhinoceroses, and many other animals are going down. These animals are in danger. Why?

• Their homes are being destroyed.

• People hunt them for their fur, horns, skins, and meat. Some are hunted for sale as pets and some because people think they are pests.

• Pollution kills them.

• Growing numbers of people crowd out animals and use up all the land and food.

• People introduce new animals to a habitat, upsetting the balance of nature.

Unless people work hard to save them, many other animals will become extinct like the dodo.

The woolly spider monkey is losing its rain forest home.

The now extinct dodo bird was the size of a large turkey. It had tiny wings that were so small it could not fly.

Why Are They Gone?

Just as you change while you grow, the world and the things that live on it change, too. Most scientists believe that the earth has changed many times in the past, and that many kinds of animals have lived on our planet.

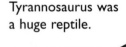

Ramphorhynchus was a flying dinosaur.

Once, there were scaly **reptiles** as big as houses. Once there were horses no bigger than cats. And, very long ago, no animals of any kind lived on land. All the animals lived in the ocean.

Dinosaurs were very important animals. They ruled the earth for more than 100 million years. They wallowed in great

Tyrannosaurus was a huge reptile.

swamps and prowled through hot, damp forests.

Then something happened, and all the dinosaurs died. We don't know why dinosaurs became **extinct**.

Brachiosaurus was a giant, plant-eating dinosaur.

Some scientists think dinosaurs became extinct slowly. Swamps began drying up. New plants were taking the place of old ones. Perhaps dinosaurs could not live with these changes. Other scientists think the earth was struck by a huge meteorite from space, and the impact caused the death of dinosaurs.

Perhaps all these things, and others that we don't know about, caused the dinosaurs and many other kinds of creatures to die. It's a great mystery.

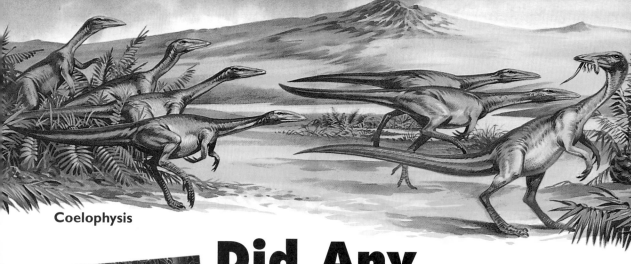

Coelophysis

A heron looks a little like the early dinosaur Coelophysis.

heron

Did Any Survive?

Of course, there were no people on the earth when dinosaurs were alive. So how do we know about dinosaurs and other animals of long ago?

Sometimes, when a dinosaur died, its body lay on the muddy ground. The soft parts rotted away, but mud covered the bones and kept them from rotting. Over millions of years, the bones and the mud turned into rock. This helped keep them whole. Over many more millions of years, sun and rain wore away the rock around it, leaving the rocky skeleton.

Smilodon

Rocky bones and skeletons are called fossils (FAHS uhlz).

Scientists look for fossils such as this and dig them out of the ground. By studying fossils, the scientists can tell what the animal looked like. They can tell what it ate by the shape of its teeth. Often, they can even tell how well the animal could see and hear and smell things.

Some creatures living in the world today look very much like some of the fossils of ancient animals. By studying these creatures, scientists can get an even better idea of life on the earth millions and millions of years ago. These two pages show some animal look-alikes.

A lioness looks a little like a Smilodon, a saber-toothed cat that lived on the earth a million years ago.

A Chance to Change

Dinosaurs were not the only prehistoric animals to become extinct. Millions of years ago, many elephantlike animals roamed the earth. Over the years, these creatures adapted to their changing environment. For example, they developed different kinds of trunks and tusks depending on what kind of food was available. Sometimes the animals could not adapt quickly enough to changes in their environment. When this happened, the animals became extinct.

moeritherium

The moeritherium was among the first elephantlike animals. It lived about 60 million years ago. The moeritherium had neither trunk nor tusks and was about as large as a pig.

The deinotherium lived between 24 million and 2 million years ago. It had backward-curving tusks that grew down from its lower jaw. Platybelodons lived

African elephant

deinotherium

during the same time as the deinotherium. They had huge scoop-shaped teeth in their lower jaws, which were probably used to pull up water plants.

Mammoths lived from at least 4 million to 10,000 years ago. They were enormous animals with teeth like those of modern-day elephants. Mammoths that lived during the Ice Age had long hair on their bodies, which helped protect them from the extreme cold.

Today, there are two kinds of elephants—the African elephant and the Indian elephant, also called the Asian elephant. In a million years, these and many of today's animals will be gone. There may be many new kinds of animals.

mammoth

Some smoke that comes from factory chimneys puts harmful chemicals into the environment.

How People Affect Animals

All around the world, every day, more people are being born. All these people need somewhere to live and work, and they need food. People take up space. They need space for their farms, their factories, their houses, and their roads. They cut down forests to make room for crops, houses, and roads. Whenever this

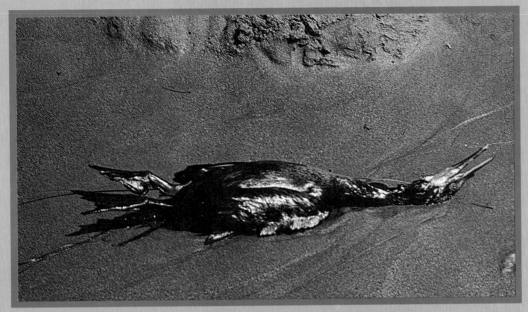

When water birds try to swim in water that is polluted with oil, they drown.

happens, animal **habitats** and homes are destroyed. Habitats are also destroyed when people pollute rivers, lakes, and forests with harmful chemicals or trash.

Tropical rain forests are home to many kinds of animals and plants. But large areas of tropical rain forests are being destroyed each year as people gather lumber, minerals, and other materials. Scientists and other people worry that if much more of the rain forests are destroyed, thousands of species of plants and animals will become extinct.

KNOW It All!

It's fun to enjoy nature, but you don't want your fun to spoil an animal's habitat. Follow these simple rules:

1. Leave plants where you find them. Do not pick wildflowers.

2. Do not take animals' eggs.

3. Keep to paths.

4. Never start fires.

5. Always take your litter home.

Too Much Hunting

Once buffalo roamed freely across many parts of North America. Because of hunting, today few buffalo are left.

Hyenas and hawks, foxes and frogs, spiders and snakes, lions and lizards, dolphins and dragonflies—all these, and many more animals, are hunters. They hunt and kill other creatures for food. Some people think such killing is cruel, but it keeps nature in balance.

People are hunters, too. They hunt for sport and for food. In many cases, hunting does not upset the balance of nature. In many countries, people are allowed to hunt only animals that are plentiful.

But some hunters kill tigers, leopards, otters, alligators, and other rare animals for their fur or skin. They sell the fur or skin to companies that make coats, shoes, belts, and purses from them. Hunters kill rhinoceroses for their horns and elephants for their tusks. They kill as many of these animals as they can for money. In many parts of the world these animals are being wiped out by hunting!

Many governments around the world have passed hunting laws to try and save animals. Hunters who break these laws and are caught have to pay huge fines—or go to prison.

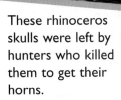

These rhinoceros skulls were left by hunters who killed them to get their horns.

Animals in Danger

Around the world, many animals are in danger of becoming extinct. This map shows just a sample.

California Condor. This large vulture requires vast areas of open, hilly country, but people are destroying its habitat. The bird has been overhunted for sport, and too many of its eggs have been collected for food. (North America)

Whooping Crane. It migrates every year. People have moved into its habitat. So few adult whooping cranes are living today that soon not enough young ones may be born. (North America)

Green Sea Turtle. It spends most of its life at sea. People eat its eggs and hunt it for its meat. (South Pacific Ocean)

Imperial Parrot. It lives in forests on tropical islands. People are destroying its habitats. Many of these birds are captured illegally and sold as pets. (South America)

Scientists say there are three main types of animals in danger. All of them need our help to survive.

Endangered animals face the most serious threat of extinction. They include the common European sturgeon, the tiger, the black rhinoceros, and the Atlantic bluefin tuna.

Vulnerable animals are sometimes called threatened animals. There are many of these animals in some areas, but their numbers are decreasing. They include the giant anteater of Central and South America, the imperial parrot, the orangutan, and the wild yak.

Lower risk animals, once called rare, either have small numbers living within a narrow area or are thinly scattered over a wider area. They include the harpy eagles of South America and the Argentine pampas deer.

Pyrenean Ibex. This graceful wild goat lives in herds along a European mountain range. Overhunting and loss of habitat have reduced its numbers. (Europe)

Giant Panda. It looks like a huge, cuddly, black-and-white toy, and it might be related to the bear. The bamboo that giant pandas eat is being cut down. (Asia)

Black Colobus. People once hunted this monkey for its black-and-white fur. Now they hunt it for food. The forests where it lives are being cut down for timber. (Africa)

Bridled Nailtail Wallaby. This small kangaroo once lived in large groups in Australia. People have moved into its habitat. Only one group of these wallabies remains. (Australia)

People to the Rescue

Many people around the world are doing all they can to help save animals

This sea otter was rescued from an oil-polluted shore. The rescue workers are cleaning it.

from becoming extinct. Zoos used to be just a collection of animals kept in cages to amuse people. Today, zoos try to keep the animals happy, too. Many animals are given large areas to live in that feel just like their homes in the wild. Zoos also breed and take care of endangered animals to save them from extinction.

Wildlife reserves and national parks are areas of land where animals and plants can live safely. There are reserves and national parks all around the world.

People help animals in other ways, too. In many countries, laws ban the hunting

The zookeeper is filing an elephant's toenails. In the wild, the nails would have worn down naturally.

or catching of certain animals. Often, when animals are put in danger by a crisis, such as an oil spill, people work around the clock to save them.

TRY THIS!

1 Show your awareness of endangered animals and have fun at the same time. Find pictures of your favorite endangered animal. Look in books, magazines, and encyclopedias. Use the pictures to help you design a mask of this animal. Use papier mâché, construction paper, buttons, yarn, or other materials to build it!

People Who Work with Animals

Do you love animals? There are many kinds of jobs for people who do. A few of those jobs are listed here.

Veterinarians, or vets, keep animals healthy. City vets deal mostly with pets, giving them shots to keep them well. Country vets take care of farm animals, such as cows and horses.

Zoologists (zoh AHL uh jihsts) study animals to find out how they live, how they get along with people and other animals, and how they change over time. Zoologists work in laboratories, zoos, or museums. Or they work at wildlife refuges in the jungle, at sea, or wherever animals live.

Zoologists must sometimes hand-feed young animals, such as these baby koalas.

Naturalists (NACH uhr uh lihsts) study nature by watching it carefully. They hike in the country to watch birds, or they visit museums, parks, and zoos. Many naturalists keep notes, sketches, and photographs of everything they see. You don't have to wait to be a grown-up to be a naturalist! Many areas have nature-study programs for children.

Game wardens and rangers help protect wild animals in national parks and game preserves. They rescue animals stranded by floods or fire and make sure people obey fishing, hunting, and camping laws.

Farmers and ranchers raise livestock that provide food for people all over the world. Farmers raise such livestock as chickens, hogs, and dairy and beef cattle. Ranchers raise sheep and cattle on huge farms.

Naturalists are people who study animals to learn more about them.

TRY THIS! 1

There are many names for people who study animals. Can you guess what each person is called?

1. I study fossils. What am I?

2. I study insects. What am I?

3. I study how animals relate to their environment. What am I?

4. I study fish. What am I?

5. I study ocean life. What am I?

6. I study mammals. What am I?

a. oceanographer
(OH shuh NAHG ruh fuhr)

b. paleontologist
(pay lee ahn TAHL uh jihst)

c. mammalogist
(ma MAHL uh jihst)

d. entomologist
(EHN tuh MAHL uh jihst)

e. ichthyologist
(IHK thee AHL uh jihst)

f. ecologist
(ee KAHL uh jihst)

Answers: 1.b; 2.d; 3.f; 4.e; 5.a; 6.c.

Glossary

Here are some of the words you read in this book. Many of them may be new to you. Some are hard to pronounce. But since you will see them again, they are good words to know. Next to each word, you will see how to say it correctly: **decomposer** (DEE kuhm POH zuhr). The part shown in small capital letters is said a little more loudly than the rest of the word. The part in large capital letters is said the loudest. Under each word are one or two sentences that tell what the word means.

A

amphibian (am FIHB ee uhn)
An amphibian is an animal that lives in water and breathes with gills when it is young. But it can live on land when it is an adult. Frogs and toads are amphibians.

arachnid (uh RAK nihd)
An arachnid is an insectlike animal with no feelers or wings. It has four pairs of jointed legs. Spiders are arachnids.

arthropod (AHR thruh pahd)
An arthropod is an animal with jointed legs and an outside shell. Insects, spiders, and crabs are arthropods.

B

bird (burd)
A bird is an animal that is warm-blooded, lays eggs, and has feathers. Sparrows are birds.

C

cold-blooded (kohld BLUHD ihd)
An animal that is cold-blooded has a body temperature that changes with the temperature of its surroundings. Snakes and lizards are cold-blooded animals.

consumer (kuhn SOOM uhr)
In a food chain, a consumer is an animal that eats plants or other animals.

D

decomposer (DEE kuhm POH zuhr)
A decomposer is a living organism that breaks down dead animals and plants into tiny parts. These parts nourish the soil and help plants grow.

E

endangered (ehn DAYN juhrd)
An endangered animal is one that is almost wiped out, or extinct. The whooping crane is an endangered animal.

extinct (ehks TINGT)
An extinct animal is one that has been destroyed, wiped out. The passenger pigeon and dodo are extinct.

F

fish (fihsh)
A fish is an animal that is cold-blooded, lives in water, and has gills. Sharks are fish.

food chain (food chayn)
A food chain is an arrangement of plants and animals in which each member feeds on the one below it in the chain. In one kind of food chain, cattle eat grass and human beings eat cattle.

gills (gihlz)
Gills are organs on the sides of fish used for breathing. They take oxygen out of the water and put oxygen into the fish's blood. Fish need gills in order to breathe.

H

habitat (HAB uh tat)
A habitat is the place where a plant or animal lives. A forest habitat may be home to fir trees, birds, and deer.

I

insect (IN sehkt)
An insect is an animal with six legs and a hard covering on its body. Butterflies, bees, and ants are insects.

invertebrate (ihn VUR tuh briht)
An invertebrate is an animal that has no backbone. A worm is an invertebrate.

M

mammal (MAM uhl)
A mammal is an animal whose young develop inside the mother's body until birth and then feed on mother's milk. Dogs, whales, bats, and human beings are mammals.

metamorphosis (MEHT uh MAWR fuh sihs)
Metamorphosis is the series of changes some animals experience as they develop. Caterpillars change into butterflies during metamorphosis.

migration (my GRAY shuhn)
Migration is an animal's movement from one place to another and back as the seasons change.

mollusk (MAHL uhsk)
A mollusk is an animal with a soft body and no bones. Many mollusks have hard shells. Clams and octopuses are mollusks.

N

naturalist (NACH uh ruh lihst)
A naturalist is a person who studies nature. Naturalists observe birds and other animals.

nectar (NEHK tuhr)
Nectar is a sweet liquid made by flowers. Nectar is eaten by some insects and gathered by bees to make honey.

O

organism (AWR guh nih zuhm)
An organism is a living thing. The tiniest plankton and the largest whales are organisms.

P

plankton (PLANGK tuhn)
Plankton is a group of small animal and plantlike living things that float or drift in water. Many types of water animals, including fish and whales, eat plankton.

pollen (PAHL uhn)
Pollen is the yellow powder inside flowers. Bees use pollen to make honey.

predator (PREHD uh tuhr)
A predator is an animal that hunts other animals. Dolphins, lions, and many insects are predators.

prey (pray)
Prey is any animal that is hunted, killed, and eaten by another animal. Insects, birds, and many mammals are prey.

producer (proh DOO suhr)
In a food chain, a producer is a plant that uses sunlight to make food. Producers are eaten by animals and other consumers.

R

reptile (REHP tuhl)
A reptile is a cold-blooded animal that creeps or crawls. Snakes and lizards are reptiles.

resource (rih SAWRS)
A resource is a supply of something that you use. It can be something that you use again and again.

S

substance (SUB stuhns)
A substance is something that you can see or feel. Pollen is a substance you find in flowers.

T

threatened (THREHT uhnd)
A threatened animal is one whose numbers are decreasing. The giant anteater is a threatened animal.

V

vertebrate (VUR tuh briht)
A vertebrate is an animal that has a backbone. Dogs, fish, and birds are vertebrates.

W

warm-blooded (wawrm BLUHD ihd)
An animal that is warm-blooded can keep a steady body temperature no matter how warm or cold its surroundings are. Mammals are warm-blooded animals.

Index

This index is an alphabetical list of important topics covered in this book. It will help you find information given in both words and pictures. To help you understand what an entry means, there is sometimes a helping word in parentheses, for example, **ajolote** (lizard). If there is information in both words and pictures, you will see the words *with pictures* in parentheses after the page number. If there is only a picture, you will see the word *picture* in parentheses after the page number.

190

Illustration Acknowledgments

The Publishers of *Childcraft* gratefully acknowledge the courtesy of the following illustrators, photographers, agencies, and organizations for illustrations in this volume. When all the illustrations for a sequence of pages are from a single source, the inclusive page numbers are given. Credits should be read from top to bottom, left to right, on their respective pages. All illustrations are the exclusive property of the publishers of *Childcraft* unless names are marked with an asterisk(*).

Cover	Tree frog—© Tim Flach, Tony Stone Images*; Centipede—Hana Sawyer; Tiger—© Michael Lewis; Viesti Associates, Inc.*; Egret—© Arthur Morris, The Stock Market*	52-53	Sheila Galbraith; Sheila Galbraith; Sheila Galbraith; © S. Nielsen, DRK*; Sheila Galbraith
Back Cover	© Michael Lewis, Viesti Associates, Inc.*	54-55	© Prato, Bruce Coleman Collection*; © Arthur Twomey, Photo Researchers*; © S. Dalton/OSF from Animals Animals*; Yoshi Miyake
1	Hana Sawyer; © Michael Lewis, Viesti Associates, Inc.*; © Arthur Morris, The Stock Market*	56-57	Mick Loates; Mick Loates; Mick Loates; Arthur Singer; © Howard G. Buffett*; Trevor Boyer
2-3	Tony Gibbons; Alex Ebel	58-59	Yoshi Miyake; Mick Loates; © Alan & Sandy Carey, Photo Researchers*; Mick Loates; Mick Loates; Mick Loates
4-5	Margaret L. Estey; Harry McNaught		
6-7	Guy Tudor; Yoshi Miyake; Walter Linsenmaier; Norman Weaver; Harry McNaught; Norman Weaver	60-61	Oxford Illustrators Ltd.; Oxford Illustrators Ltd.; Oxford Illustrators Ltd.; Mick Loates; Oxford Illustrators Ltd.; Oxford Illustrators Ltd.; Oxford Illustrators Ltd.;
8-9	Alan Male; Wayne Stuart; WORLD BOOK illustration by Robert Hynes; WORLD BOOK illustration; Eraldo Carugati and George Lopac	62-63	Mick Loates; Oxford Illustrators Ltd.; Oxford Illustrators Ltd.; Harry McNaught; Stephen Brayfield; Harry McNaught; Harry McNaught; Harry McNaught; Oxford Illustrators Ltd.
10-11	Yoshi Miyake; Hana Sawyer; Jan Wills; Allan Roberts; © Howard G. Buffett*; © Howard G. Buffett*	64-65	Pamela G. Johnson; Patricia Wayne; © Dan Suzio, Animals Animals*; © Lars Christiansen, APF*
12-13	Pamela G. Johnson; Walter Linsenmaier; WORLD BOOK illustration; WORLD BOOK illustration; James Teason; E. R. Degginger	66-67	Harry McNaught
14-15	Guy Tudor; Pamela G. Johnson; Jean Cassels	68-69	Alan Male; Alan Male; Alan Male; © C. Prescott-Allen, Animals Animals*
16-17	Jean Cassels; © Howard G. Buffett*; Jean Cassels	70-71	Oxford Illustrators Ltd.
18-19	© Anthony Healy, Bruce Coleman Collection*; © Jane Burton, Bruce Coleman Collection*; Judy Hierstein	72-73	© Jane Burton, Bruce Coleman Collection*; © Adrian Davies*; © Hans Reinhard, Bruce Coleman Collection*
20-21	Pedro Julio Gongales; © Konrad Wothe, ENP Images*; Robert Morton	74-75	© C. B. & D. W. Firth, Bruce Coleman Collection.*; © John Visser, Bruce Coleman Inc.*; © Raymond A. Mendez, Photo Trends*; Robert Masheris
22-23	Eileen Mueller Neill	76-77	© Leonard Lee Rue III/NAS from Photo Researchers*; Harry McNaught; © Joe McDonald, Tom Stack & Associates*; © George Bernard, Animals Animals*
24-25	Peter Snowball		
26-27	© Lawrence Migdale, Tony Stone Images*; Yoshi Miyake		
28-29	Lydia Halverson; Eileen Mueller Neill	78-79	© E. R. Degginger, Animals Animals*; © Leonard Lee Rue, Bruce Coleman Inc.*
30-31	Linda Liefer; Walter Linsenmaier	80-81	CHILDCRAFT illustration; Alan Male; Harry McNaught
32-33	Norman Weaver; Roberta Polfus; Alex Ebel; Norman Weaver	82-83	© Armstrong, Zefa Picture Library*; © Hans Reinhard, Bruce Coleman Collection*; © Layer, Zefa Picture Library*; Peter Snowball; Harry McNaught
34-35	J. M. Conrader*; G. J. Chafaris*; Graham Allen, Linden Artists Ltd.; Jean Cassels		
36-37	© Leonard Lee Rue III, Bruce Coleman Collection*; Roberta Polfus; © Jen & Des Bartlett, Bruce Coleman Inc.*; Jean Cassels	84-85	© George Porter/NAS from Photo Researchers*; © Jane Burton, Bruce Coleman Collection*
		86-87	Yoshi Miyake; Roberta Polfus
38-39	Peter Visscher; © Hans Reinhard, Bruce Coleman Collection*; © Lothar Lenz/Okapia from Photo Researchers*	88-89	E. R. Degginger; © G. Ronald Austing*; © Leonard Lee Rue III, APF*; © G. Ronald Austing*
40-41	Maureen Hallahan; Darrell Wiskur; Peter Snowball; Samantha Smith	90-91	Norman Weaver; Tony Gibbons; Norman Weaver; Norman Weaver
42-43	© Kim Taylor, Bruce Coleman Collection*; Richard Orr; Michael Hague	92-93	Yoshi Miyake
		94-95	Tony Gibbons; © Giorgio Gualco, Bruce Coleman Collection*
44-45	Eileen Mueller Neill	96-97	© Norbert Wu*; © Zig Leszczynski, Animals Animals*; Norman Weaver
46-47	Trevor Boyer; © Ken Balcomb, Bruce Coleman Collection*; Donald C. Meighan; WORLD BOOK illustration; WORLD BOOK illustration; WORLD BOOK illustration	98-99	© Paul A. Zahl, Photo Researchers*; © Denise Tackett, Tom Stack & Associates*
48-49	James Teason; Colin Newman		
50-51	Guy Tudor; Guy Tudor; Guy Tudor; Trevor Boyer; Alex Ebel		